Quantitative Data Analysis Using SPSS

Quantitative Data Analysis Using SPSS

An Introduction for Health & Social Science

Pete Greasley

Open University Press

Open University Press
McGraw-Hill Education
McGraw-Hill House
Shoppenhangers Road
Maidenhead
Berkshire
England
SL6 2QL

email: enquiries@openup.co.uk
world wide web: www.openup.co.uk

and Two Penn Plaza, New York, NY 10121-2289, USA

First published 2008

A catalogue record of this book is available from the British Library

ISBN-10: 0 335 22305 2 (pb)   0 335 22306 0 (hb)
ISBN-13: 978 0335 22305 3 (pb)   978 0335 22306 0 (hb)

Library of Congress Cataloging-in-Publication Data
CIP data applied for

Typeset by RefineCatch Limited, Bungay, Suffolk
Printed in the UK by Bell and Bain Ltd, Glasgow

The *McGraw·Hill* Companies

Contents

Introduction

I remember reading somewhere that for every mathematical formula, included in a book, the sales would be reduced by half. So guess what, there are no formulas, equations or mathematical calculations in this book. This is a *practical* introduction to quantitative data analysis using the most widely available statistical software – SPSS (Statistical Package for the Social Sciences). The aim is to get students and professionals past that first hurdle of dealing with quantitative data analysis and statistics.

The book is based upon a simple scenario: a local doctor has conducted a brief patient satisfaction questionnaire about the counselling service offered at his health centre. The doctor, having no knowledge of quantitative data analysis, sends the data from 30 questionnaires to you, the researcher, for analysis.

The book begins by exploring the types of data that are produced from this questionnaire and the types of analysis that may be conducted on the data. The subsequent chapters explain how to enter the data into SPSS and conduct the various types of analyses in a very simple step-by-step format, just as a researcher might proceed in practice.

Each of the chapters should take about an hour to complete the analysis and exercises. So, in principle, the basic essentials of quantitative data analysis and SPSS may be mastered in a matter of just six hours of independent study. The chapters are listed below with a brief synopsis of their content.

- *Chapter 1 A questionnaire and what to do with it: types of data and relevant analyses.* The aim of this chapter is to familiarize yourself with the questionnaire and the types of analyses that may be conducted on the data.
- *Chapter 2 Coding the data for SPSS, setting up an SPSS database and entering data.* In this chapter you will learn how to code the data for SPSS, set up an SPSS database and enter the data from 30 questionnaires.
- *Chapter 3 Descriptive statistics: frequencies, measures of central tendency and visually illustrating data using graphs.* In this chapter you will use SPSS to produce some basic descriptive statistics from the data: frequencies for categorical data and measures of central tendency (the mean, median and mode) for interval level data. You will also learn how to produce and edit charts to illustrate the data analysis, and to copy your work into a Microsoft Word file.
- *Chapter 4 Cross-tabulation and the chi-square statistic.* In this chapter you will learn about cross-tabulation for categorical data, a statistical test (chi-square) to examine associations between variables, and the concept of statistical significance. You will also learn how to re-code interval data into categories.
- *Chapter 5 Correlation: examining relationships between interval data.* In this

chapter you will learn about scatterplots and correlation to examine the direction and strength of relationships between variables.

- *Chapter 6   Examining differences between two sets of scores.* In this chapter you will learn about tests which tell us if there is a statistically significant difference between two sets of scores. In so doing you will learn about independent and dependent variables, parametric and non-parametric data, and independent and related samples.

There is also a final concluding chapter which provides advice on how to structure the report of a quantitative study and how *not* to present data.

The approach

Quantitative data analysis and statistics is often a frightening hurdle for many students in the health and social sciences, so my primary concern has been to make the book as simple and accessible as possible. This quest for simplicity starts with the fact that the student has only one dataset to familiarize themselves with – and that dataset itself is very simple: a patient satisfaction questionnaire consisting of just five questions.

The questionnaire is, however, designed to yield a range of statistical analyses and should hopefully illustrate the potentially complex levels of analyses that can arise from just a few questions. This will also act as a warning to students who embark upon research projects involving complex designs without fully appreciating how they will actually analyse the data. My advice to students who are new to research is always to 'keep it simple' and, where possible, to design the study according to the statistics they understand.

I have taken a pragmatic approach to quantitative data analysis which means that I have focused on the practicalities of doing the analyses rather than ruminating on the theoretical underpinnings of statistical principles. And since actually doing the analyses requires knowledge of appropriate statistical software, I have chosen to illustrate this using the most widely available and comprehensive statistical package in universities: SPSS. Thus, by the end of this book you should not only be able to select the appropriate statistical test for the data, you should also be able to conduct the analysis and produce the results using SPSS.

The scope of the book

I have set a distinct limit to the level of analysis which I think is appropriate for an introductory text. This limit is the analyses of two variables – known as bi-variate analyses. In my experience of teaching health and social science students, most of whom are new to quantitative data analysis and statistics, this is sufficient for an introduction.

Also, I did not want to scare people off with a more imposing tome covering things like *logistic regression* and *factorial ANOVA*. There are many other books which include these more advanced statistics, some of which are listed in the references. This book is designed to get people started with quantitative data analysis using SPSS; as such it may provide a platform for readers to consult these texts with more confidence.

The audience: health and social sciences

As an introduction to quantitative data analysis, this book should be relevant to undergraduates, postgraduates or diploma level students undertaking a first course in quantitative research methods. I have used these materials to teach students from a variety of backgrounds including health, social sciences and management.

It may be particularly relevant for students and professionals in health and social care, partly due to the subject matter (a patient satisfaction question-naire about counselling) and the examples used throughout the text, but also due to the design of the materials. Many students and professionals in health and social care are studying part-time or by distance learning, or per-haps undertaking short courses in research methods. This means that their opportunities for attendance are often limited and courses need to be designed to cater for this mode of study, for example, attendance for one or two days at a time.

It is with these students in mind that these materials should also be suitable for independent study. After the introductory chapter outlining the types of data and analyses, the book continues with step-by-step instructions for con-ducting the analysis using SPSS. Furthermore, the practical approach should suit professionals who may wish to develop their own proposals and conduct their own research but have limited time to delve into the theoretical details of statistical principles.

In health studies the emphasis on evidence-based practice has reinforced the need for professionals to not only understand and critically appraise the research evidence but also to conduct research in their own areas of practice. This book should provide professionals with a basic knowledge of the principles of quantitative research along with the means to actually design and conduct the analysis of data using SPSS.

For lecturers

This book is an organized course divided into six chapters/sessions which may be delivered as a combination of lectures and practical sessions on SPSS. I have delivered this course in three ways:

1 First, as a series of five weekly lectures and practical sessions (two–three hours) for the first half of a postgraduate module on quantitative and qualitative data analysis.

   The first session primarily consists of a lecture introducing the question-naire, the dataset and relevant analyses (Chapter 1) before moving on to enter the data (Chapter 2). Thereafter, each of the remaining four sessions consists of an introductory lecture discussing the analysis in subsequent chapters (descriptive statistics and graphs, cross-tabulation and chi-square, correlation, examining differences in two sets of scores) before moving onto SPSS to conduct the analyses and exercises in each chapter. In the final session I also include discussion of writing up the results and reporting more generally (Chapter 7).

For a full module of 10–11 sessions this book could either be supplemented by additional materials covering more advanced analyses (e.g., ANOVA and regression analysis) or students could design (and conduct) their own study (in groups) based upon the analyses covered in the book.

2 A one/two day course for a postgraduate module on Research Methods. This starts with formal lecture introducing the questionnaire, the dataset and relevant analyses (Chapter 1), and then students (in pairs) work through the materials at their own pace, continuing with independent study. The practical sessions may be interspersed with brief lectures reviewing the types of analyses.

3 A half-day workshop on SPSS. Again, this begins with a brief introduction to the questionnaire, the dataset and types of analyses, with guided instruction on specific exercises from each of the chapters. Though it has to be said that a half day is not really sufficient time to cover the materials (in my view, and according to the student evaluations!) This is especially the case for students with little prior knowledge of statistics.

Where an assignment has been set for the course, students have been asked to produce a report for the doctor who requested the analysis. This requires students to write a structured report in which the 'most relevant analyses' are presented along with some discussion of the results, critical reflections on the survey and recommendations for further research.

Getting a copy of SPSS

SPSS, as noted above, is the most widely used software for the statistical analysis of quantitative data. It is available for use at most universities where staff and students can usually purchase their own copy on CD for £10–£20. The licence, which expires at the end of each year, can be renewed by contacting the supplier at the university who will provide the necessary 'authorization' code.

Acknowledgements

Thanks to all the students who have endured evolving versions of this text, to the publishing people for coping with the numerous figures and screenshots, and to Wendy Calvert (proof-reader extraordinaire).

A questionnaire and what to do with it: types of data and relevant analyses

The aim of this chapter is to familiarize yourself with the questionnaire and the types of analyses that may be conducted on the data before we go onto SPSS. By the end of the chapter you should be familiar with: types of data and levels of measurement; frequencies and cross-tabulation; measures of central tendency; normal and skewed distributions of data; correlation and scatterplots; independent and dependent variables.

1.1 The questionnaire

A local general practice (family practice or health centre for those outside the UK) has been offering a counselling service to patients for over a year now. The doctor at the practice refers patients to a counsellor if they are suffering from mild to moderate mental health issues, like anxiety or depression.[1]

The doctor decided that he wanted to evaluate the service by gathering some information about the patients referred for counselling and their satisfaction with the service. So, he designed a brief questionnaire and sent it to every patient who attended for counselling over the year. The doctor had referred 30 patients to the service and was delighted to find that all 30 returned the questionnaire.

But then he realized he had a bit of a problem – he did not know how to analyse the data! That is when he thought of you. So, with a polite accompanying letter appealing for help, he sends you the 30 completed questionnaires for analysis. A copy of the questionnaire is provided in Figure 1.1.

The first thing you notice is that he has collected some basic demographic data about the gender and age of the patients. Then you see that he has asked whether they saw the male or female counsellor – that might be interesting in terms of satisfaction ratings: perhaps one received higher ratings than the other? He has also collected information about the number of counselling sessions conducted for each patient because, he tells you in the letter, the counsellors are supposed to offer 'brief therapy' averaging six sessions. Are they both abiding by this? Finally, you see that patients were asked to rate their satisfaction with the service on a seven point scale. Will the ratings depend on the sex or age of the patient? Perhaps they would be related to the number of counselling sessions or, as noted above, which particular counsellor the patient saw.

Well, you think, that is not too bad – at least it is simple. But what sorts of analysis can you do on this questionnaire? (See Box 1.1 for a brief discussion of some questionnaire design issues.)

Patient Satisfaction Questionnaire	
Q1. Sex:	Male ❑ Female ❑
Q2. Age:	Age: .... (years)
Q3. Which counsellor did you see?	John ❑ Jane ❑
Q4. Number of counselling sessions?	.... (number)
Q5. Satisfaction with service: Please indicate the extent to which you were satisfied with the service on the following scale by circling the appropriate number: Not at all satisfied 1 2 3 4 5 6 7 Very satisfied	

Figure 1.1 Counselling service: patient satisfaction questionnaire

Box 1.1 Questionnaires: some design issues

While this is not the place for a full discussion of questionnaire design issues, there are some cardinal rules that should be briefly noted.

First, make sure the questions are clear, brief and unambiguous. In particular avoid 'double questions', for example: 'Was the room in which the counselling took place quiet and comfortable? Well, it was comfortable but there was a lot of noise from the next room . . .'

Second, make sure that the questionnaire is easy to complete by using 'closed questions' with check boxes providing the relevant options that respondents can simply tick. So, you should avoid questions like: 'Q79: Please list all the times you felt anxious, where you were, who you were with, and what you'd had to eat the night before'.

The more you think through the options before, the less work there will be later when it comes round to analysing the data. As Robson (2002: 245) points out: 'The desire to use open-ended questions appears to be almost universal in novice survey researchers, but is usually extinguished with experience . . .' Piloting the questionnaire, which is important to check how respondents may interpret the questions, can also provide suggestions for closed alternatives.

There are some occasions, however, when 'open questions' are necessary to provide useful information. For example, the question about level of satisfaction with the service may have benefited from a comments box to allow patients to expand on issues relating to satisfaction. An alternative strategy may have been to use more scales to measure different dimensions of satisfaction (for example, relating to the counsellor, the room in which counselling was conducted, the referral procedure, etc.)

Another issue is the design of the scale used to measure satisfaction. The doctor might have used a more typical Likert-type format where the respondent indicates the extent to which they agree or disagree with a statement:

I was satisfied with the service:

Strongly disagree	Disagree	Undecided	Agree	Strongly agree
☐	☐	☐	☐	☐

Notice that there are only five options here (and they are labelled). The format you use will depend on the context and the level of sensitivity you require, which may result in a seven or nine point scale. Also notice that whatever the length of the scale, there is an option for a 'neutral' or 'undecided' response.

In the counselling questionnaire you may also notice that the question asking for the age of patients may have provided a list of age groupings, for example, 20–9, 30–9. Although categories can make the questionnaire easier to complete, and more anonymous (some people may not like to specify their age because it may help to identify them), my advice would be to gather the precise ages where possible because you can convert them into any categories you want later; the same principle applies to number of counselling sessions.

A full discussion of questionnaire design issues would require a chapter unto itself. For further reading Robson (2002) provides a relatively succinct chapter with guidance on design and other issues.

1.2 What types of analyses can we perform on this questionnaire?

1.2.1 Descriptive statistics

Descriptive statistics provide summary information about data, for example, the number of patients who are male or female, or the average age of patients. There are three distinct types of data that are important for statistical analysis:

Types of data (or levels of measurement)

1 *Interval or Ratio*: This is data which takes the form of a scale in which the numbers go from low to high in equal intervals. Height and weight are obvious examples. In our data this applies to age, number of counselling sessions and patient satisfaction ratings.

2 *Ordinal*: This is data that can be put into an ordered sequence. For example, the rank order of runners in a race – 1st, 2nd, 3rd, etc. Notice that this gives no information on how much quicker 1st was than 2nd or 2nd was than 3rd. So, in a race, the winner may have completed the course in 20 seconds, the runner-up in 21 seconds, but third place may have taken 30 seconds. Whereas there is only one second difference between 1st and 2nd, there are nine seconds difference between second and third. Do we have any of this type of data in our sample? No we do not (though see Box 1.2 for further discussion).

3 *Categorical or nominal*: This is data that represents different categories, rather than a scale. In our data this applies to: sex (male or female) and counsellor (John or Jane). So, if we were assigning numbers to these categories, as we will be doing, they do not have any order as they would have

in a scale: if we were to code male as 1 and female as 2, this does not imply any order to the numbers – it is just an arbitrary assignment of numbers to categories.

Making a distinction between these levels of measurement is important because *the type of analysis we can perform on the data from the questionnaire depends on the type of data* – as illustrated in Table 1.1.

Table 1.1 Type of data and appropriate descriptive statistics

Type of data	Descriptive statistics
Categorical data:	Frequencies, cross-tabulation.
Interval/ratio data:	Measures of central tendency: mean, median, mode.

We will now examine each of these in turn.

Box 1.2 Types of data & levels of measurement

Whereas this brief review is really all we need to know for our questionnaire data, there is in fact a lot more to say about types of data and levels of measurement. For example, although I have grouped interval and ratio data together, as many textbooks do (e.g., Bryman and Cramer 2001: 57), there is much debate about the differences between true interval data and that provided in rating scales.

In our questionnaire, age and counselling sessions are ratio data because there is a true zero point and we know that someone who is 40 years is twice as old as someone who is 20 years; similarly, we know that 12 counselling sessions is four times as many as three; we know the ratio of scores. The problem with interval data is that, while the intervals may be equal we cannot be sure that the ratio of scores is equal. For example, if we were measuring anxiety on a scale of 0–100, should we maintain that a person who scored 80 had twice as much anxiety as a person who scored 40? (Howell 1997: 6.)

This issue could be raised about our satisfaction ratings: can we really be sure that a patient who circles 6 is twice as satisfied as a person who circles 3, or three times as satisfied as a person who circles 2? It is for this reason that some analysts would treat this as ordinal data – like the rank order of runners in a race – 1st, 2nd, 3rd, etc. described above. But clearly, our satisfaction rating scale is more than ordinal, and since the numerical intervals in the scale are presented as equal (assuming equal intervals between the numbers) we might say they 'approximate' interval data.

For those who wish to delve further into this debate about whether rating scales should be treated as ordinal or interval data see Howell (1997) or the recent articles in *Medical Education* by Jamieson (2004) and Pell (2005).

Descriptive statistics for categorical data

Frequencies. Probably the first thing a researcher would do with the data from our questionnaire is to 'run some frequencies'. This simply means that we would look at the numbers and percentages for our categorical questions, which we might hereafter refer to as 'variables' (because the data may *vary* according to the patient answering the question: male/female, old/young, satisfied or not satisfied etc.)

- How many males/females were referred for counselling? Are they similar proportions? Were there more males or females?
- How many patients were seen by John and how many were seen by Jane? Did they both see a similar number of patients?

Cross-tabulation. The next step might be to cross-tabulate this data to gain more specific information about the relationship between these two variables. For example, imagine that we had collected this information for 200 patients and, from our frequencies analysis on each variable, we found the following results:

Table 1.2 Sex of patients

	Number	Percent
Male	100	50%
Female	100	50%
Total	200	100%

Table 1.3 Counsellor seen by patients

	Number	Percent
John	100	50%
Jane	100	50%
Total	200	100%

While these tables tell us that 50 per cent of patients were male, and that each counsellor saw 50 per cent of patients, they do not inform us about the *relationship* between the two variables: were the male and female patients equally distributed across the two counsellors or, at the other extreme, did all the female patients see Jane and all the male patients see John? In order to find this out we need to cross-tabulate the data. It might produce the following table:

Table 1.4 Cross-tabulation of gender and counsellor

	John	Jane	Total
Male	80	20	100
Female	20	80	100
Total	100	100	200

In this example we can see that there were 100 male and 100 female patients (row totals). We can also see that the counsellors saw an equal number of patients: 100 saw John and 100 saw Jane (column totals). However, this cross-tabulation table also shows us that patients were not equally distributed across the two counsellors: whereas 80 per cent of males saw John, 80 per cent of females saw Jane. If the patients were randomly distributed to each of the counsellors you would expect a similar proportion seeing each of the counsellors. So in this hypothetical example it would appear that there is some preference for male patients to see a male counsellor, and for females to see a female counsellor.

This might be important information for the doctor. For example, if one of the counsellors was intending to leave and the doctor needed to employ another counsellor, this might suggest is it necessary to ensure a male and a female counsellor are available to cater for patient preferences.

Descriptive statistics for interval data: Measures of central tendency

Having 'run frequencies' and cross-tabulated our categorical variables, we would next turn to the other variables that contain *interval data*: age, number of counselling sessions and satisfaction ratings. If we wanted to produce summary information about these items it would be more useful to provide measures of central tendency: means, medians or modes.

The Mean. The arithmetic mean is the most common measure of central tendency. It is simply the sum of the scores divided by the number of scores. So, to calculate the mean in the following example, we simply divide the sum of the ages by the number of patients: $355/11 = 32$. Thus, the mean age of the patients is 32 years.

Table 1.5 Calculating the mean age

Patient:	1	2	3	4	5	6	7	8	9	10	11	Sum
Age:	46	23	34	25	28	31	23	40	36	45	24	355

The Median. The median is another common measure of central tendency. It is the midpoint of an ordered distribution of scores. Thus, if we *order the age of patients from lowest to highest* it looks like this:

Table 1.6 Finding the median age

Patient:	1	2	3	4	5	6	7	8	9	10	11
Age:	23	23	24	25	28	31	34	36	40	45	46

The median is simply the middle number, in this case 31.

If you have an even number of cases – with no singular middle number then you just take the midpoint between those two numbers:

Table 1.7 Finding the median age in an even number of cases

Patient:	1	2	3	4	5	6	7	8	9	10
Age:	23	23	24	25	28	31	34	46	40	45

You then simply calculate the midpoint between these two central values: $(28+31)/2 = 29.5$

The Mode. The mode, which is generally of less use, is simply the most frequently occurring value. In our age example above that would be 23 – since it occurs twice – all the other ages only occur once. As an example, the mode might be useful for a shoe manufacturer who wanted to know the most common shoe size of the population.

When should I refer to the mean or the median? In the data above, which provided the ages of 11 patients (Tables 1.5 and 1.6), we saw that the mean value was 32 years and the median age was just one year younger at 31 years. So the two values are very similar. However, in some data the mean and the median values might be quite different. Consider the following example which shows the salary of employees at a small company:

Table 1.8 Salary of employees at a small company

Employee:	1	2	3	4	5	6	7	8	9	Total
Salary:	8,000	8,000	9,000	9,000	**10,000**	11,000	11,000	40,000	45,000	151,000

Here, whereas the median salary is £10,000, the mean actually works out at: £151,000/9 = £16,777. This is clearly not representative as a measure of central tendency since the majority of employees (seven out of nine) get well below the mean salary! From this example, we can see how a couple of extreme values can distort the mean value of a dataset. In such cases we should cite the median which is more representative.

Darrell Huff (1991), in his classic short book *How to Lie with Statistics*, points out that this ambiguity in the common use of the term 'average' (a more-or-less typical centre value) is a common ploy in the deceptive use of statistics. For example, a magazine may choose to cite the larger mean (rather than median) income of their readers to make it look like they have a wealthier readership, thus encouraging more advertising revenue. In statistical terms the 'average' will invariably be used to refer to the arithmetic mean.

The normal distribution. Statistically speaking, the mean should be used when the data is normally distributed. For example, if we survey 30 people coming out of a supermarket we might expect that there would be a few very young and very old shoppers, but most people would be aged between, say, 30–60 years. This is illustrated in Figure 1.2.

Here we can see that most people are aged between 30 and 60, and the mean value and median value are virtually identical: mean age = 40.5 years; median age = 40 years.

However, when the data is not normally distributed, when it is skewed towards the lower or higher end, the mean and the median values are not equivalent. So, if we turn back to our employee salaries example (with a larger set of fictitious data), where a few employees get very high salaries, we might find a distribution like the one illustrated in Figure 1.3.

This is known as a skewed distribution because the data is skewed to one end of the scale – in this case it is 'skewed off' towards the higher end of the salary scale – whereas the salary for most people, as illustrated by the median value, is at this lower end of the scale.

It is important that we examine the spread of interval data to see whether the mean or the median is the most valid measure of central tendency. If we have

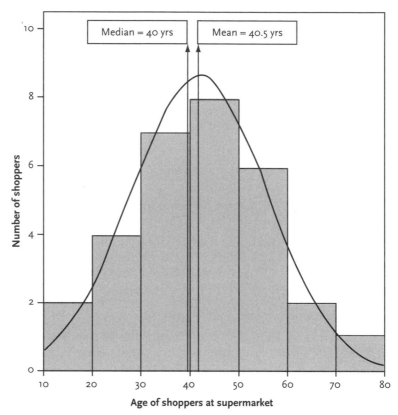

Figure 1.2 Supermarket shoppers: age normally distributed

data that is markedly skewed, then the mean value may not be a reliable measure. We shall see later that a 'normal' or skewed distribution can also dictate
which statistical test we should use to analyse the data.

Section summary

We have thus far considered the various ways of *describing* the data from the
doctor's questionnaire. We have seen that categorical data may be described
using frequencies and cross-tabulation, and that interval data may be
described using measures of central tendency: the mean, median and mode.
We have also seen that the validity of citing the mean or the median depends
on the distribution of the data. Where it is normally distributed the mean can
be used, but when data is extremely skewed to one end of the scale, the median
may be a more reliable measure of central tendency.

How might we apply this to our counselling data? Well, we might want to
summarize our interval data to answer the following questions:

• What was the mean age of patients seen for counselling?
• What was the mean number of sessions?
• Were most patients satisfied with the service? What was the mean score?

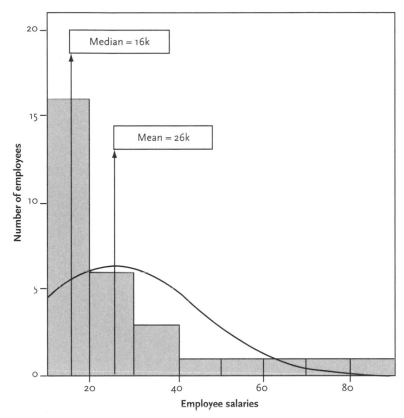

Figure 1.3 Employee salaries: skewed distribution

Notice that I have referred to mean values in the above questions. The most appropriate measure of central tendency should of course be used – the mean or the median – and this will depend on the spread of the data. It is not unusual to find that both are cited to demonstrate the reliability of the mean – or otherwise.

1.2.2 Relationships and differences in the data

There are two further types of analyses that we might conduct on interval data:

• Examine the *relationship* between variables.
• Examine *differences* between two sets of scores.

Examining relationships between variables with interval data: correlation

We have already looked at the relationship between items with *categorical* data using cross-tabulation. For variables with interval data – such as age – we can use another technique known as correlation.

A correlation illustrates the direction and strength of a relationship between two variables. For example, we might expect that height and shoe size are related – that taller people have larger feet.

Figure 1.4 shows a scatterplot of height and shoe size for 30 people, where we can see that, as height increases, so does shoe size. This is known as a positive correlation: the more tightly the plot forms a line rising from left to right, the stronger the correlation.

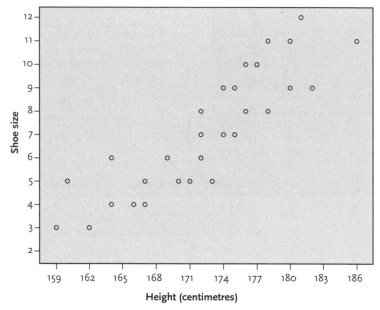

Figure 1.4 Positive correlation between height and shoe size

A negative correlation is the opposite: high scores on one variable are linked with low scores on another. For example, we might find a negative correlation between IQ scores and the number of hours spent each week watching reality TV shows, as illustrated in Figure 5.1 (hypothetical data).

From this scatterplot we can discern a line descending from left to right in the opposite direction to the height and shoe size plot.

Finally, we would probably not expect to find an association between IQ and shoe size, as illustrated in Figure 1.6, where there is no discernible correlation between the two variables.[2]

In Chapter 5 we will look at how to produce these scatterplots in SPSS.

How might we apply this to our counselling data? Well, first of all we need to identify two interval variables that might be correlated. We have three to choose from: age, number of counselling sessions and satisfaction ratings.

So, as one example, we might want to see if patients' satisfaction ratings are linked to the number of appointments they had. Perhaps the more

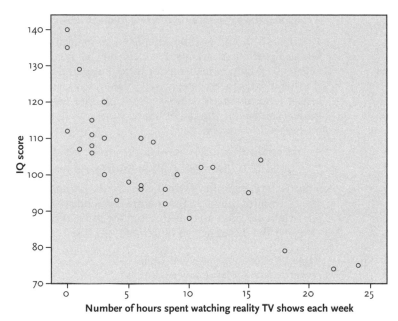

Figure 1.5 Negative correlation between IQ and interest in reality TV shows

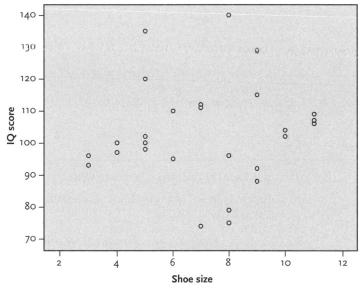

Figure 1.6 Scatterplot for IQ and shoe size

appointments they had the more satisfied they were? Or maybe this is wrong: perhaps more appointments are linked to more unresolved problems and thus less satisfaction?

Examining the differences in scores within variables

Finally, we should also be interested in examining any differences in scores *within* a particular variable. For example, we might wish to calculate the mean satisfaction ratings achieved for John compared to those for Jane. If we were to do this it is useful to categorize variables into two kinds: *independent variables* and *dependent variables*. So, if we think that level of satisfaction depends on which counsellor the patient saw, we would have the following *independent* and *dependent variables*:

- *Independent variable*: counsellor (John or Jane).
- *Dependent variable*: satisfaction rating.

Thus we are examining whether patients satisfaction ratings are *dependent* on the counsellor they saw. For example, if each counsellor saw five patients, then we would calculate the mean score for John and the mean score for Jane and consider the difference, as illustrated in Table 1.9.

Table 1.9 Comparing mean satisfaction ratings for John and Jane (hypothetical data)

	John	Jane
	2	5
	3	4
	4	7
	2	6
	3	5
Sum	14	27
Mean	2.8	5.4

In Chapter 6 we will use a statistic that tells us whether or not any difference in the two mean scores is *statistically significant*, which basically means that it was unlikely to have occurred by chance.

Summary

That is the end of this first chapter in which you have learned about:

- Different types of data and levels of measurement (categorical, ordinal and interval data).
- Frequencies and cross-tabulation.
- Measures of central tendency – mean, median and mode.
- Appropriate use of the mean or the median value depending on the distribution of the data – is it normally distributed or skewed to one end of the scale?
- Using scatterplots to see if interval data is correlated.
- Categorizing variables into independent variables and dependent variables to examine differences between two sets of scores.

Having familiarized ourselves with the dataset and the types of analysis we may conduct on it, we now need to enter the data into SPSS. That is, after you have completed the exercises . . .

1.4 Exercises

Exercise 1.1 Types of data

Would the following variables yield interval or nominal/categorical data?

(a) ethnic background;
(b) student assignment marks;
(c) level of education;
(d) patient satisfaction ratings on a 1–7 scale.

Exercise 1.2 Measures of central tendency

Which do you imagine would be the most representative measure of central tendency for the following data?

(a) number of days taken by students at a University to return overdue library books;
(b) IQ scores for a random sample of the population;
(c) number of patients cured of migraine in a year by an acupuncturist;
(d) number of counselling sessions attended by patients.

Exercise 1.3 Correlation

What sort of correlation would you expect to see from the following variables?

(a) fuel bills and temperature;
(b) ice-cream sales and temperature;
(c) number of counselling sessions and gender.

Exercise 1.4 Independent and dependent variables

Identify the independent and dependent variables in the following research questions:

(a) Does alcohol affect a person's ability to calculate mathematical problems?
(b) Is acupuncture better than physiotherapy in treating back pain?

Exercise 1.5 What type of analysis?

What type of analysis would you perform to examine the following?

(a) relationship between gender and preference for a cat or dog as a pet;
(b) relationship between time spent on an assignment and percentage mark;
(c) relationship between gender and patient satisfaction ratings.

You will find answers to the exercises at the end of the book.

1.5 Notes

1   Mental health issues are the third most common reason for consulting a general practitioner (GP), after respiratory disorders and cardiovascular disorders. A quarter of routine GP consultations relate to people with a mental health problem, most commonly depression and anxiety. It has been estimated that over half the general practices in England (51%) provide counselling services for patients (for further details and references see Greasley and Small 2005a).

2   While we might not expect to find a correlation between IQ and shoe size in a random sample of 30 people, there may be some samples for which we might find a correlation, for example, relating to age differences.

2 Coding the data for SPSS, setting up an SPSS database and entering the data

In this chapter you will learn how to code the data for SPSS, set up an SPSS database and enter the data.

2.1 The dataset

The data from the 30 questionnaires is provided in Table 2.1. Each row provides data for that particular patient: their sex and age, the counsellor they saw, how many sessions they attended, and their satisfaction rating for the counselling.

Table 2.1 Data from the counselling satisfaction questionnaire

Patient	Sex	Age	Counsellor	Sessions	Satisfaction
1	male	21	John	8	5
2	male	22	John	8	4
3	male	25	John	9	7
4	female	36	Jane	6	2
5	male	41	Jane	4	1
6	female	28	Jane	5	3
7	male	26	John	12	5
8	female	38	Jane	7	3
9	male	35	John	10	5
10	male	24	John	11	6
11	female	41	Jane	6	4
12	female	34	Jane	9	5
13	male	32	John	9	4
14	female	38	Jane	5	1
15	male	33	John	12	5
16	female	42	Jane	7	5
17	male	31	John	5	4
18	male	33	John	8	6
19	female	40	John	8	6
20	female	47	Jane	9	7
21	female	27	Jane	6	4
22	male	44	Jane	6	3
23	female	43	John	3	5
24	female	33	Jane	7	3
25	female	45	John	10	2
26	male	36	Jane	7	5
27	female	49	John	8	4
28	female	39	Jane	6	4
29	male	35	Jane	7	4
30	female	38	Jane	3	2

2.2 Coding the data for SPSS

We now need to enter our data from Table 2.1 into SPSS. This will enable us to conduct all the analyses discussed in the previous chapter – frequencies, cross-tabulation, measures of central tendency (mean, median, mode), correlations, graphs, etc., at the click of a button (well, a few buttons in some cases).

But before we can enter the data into SPSS we need to give our variables names and code the data – because all data in SPSS should be entered as numbers. The simplest way to illustrate this is through the codebook I have produced for the data in Figure 2.1.

The first column provides the variable name that we will use for SPSS. In the second column I have written some coding instructions. Since all our data needs to be entered as numbers, this means that data which is not collected as numbers, like male/female, needs to be converted into numbers. For example, in our codebook, we have assigned the number 1 for male, and 2 for female.[1]

SPSS variable name	Coding instructions
Patient	Number assigned to each patient/questionnaire. It is important to assign a number to each patient for three reasons: 1 In case you need to refer to the actual questionnaire to check the data for that patient. 2 In case you need to add more data for that patient from a further questionnaire at a later date. 3 In SPSS it is sometimes useful to re-order or 'sort' the data, for example, by putting all the males together at the top of the file. Without patient numbers you would be unable to 'sort' the file back into its original order!
Sex	1 = male 2 = female
Age	Age in years
Counsellor	1 = John 2 = Jane
Sessions	Enter number of sessions
Satisfaction	Enter satisfaction rating 1–7

Figure 2.1 An SPSS codebook for the data in Table 2.1

In practice, for a questionnaire with only five questions and only two coded variables, the idea of producing a codebook is a little excessive. But for larger questionnaires it can be a very useful reference point. Alternatively, another strategy is to simply add any codes for categorical variables on a copy of the questionnaire so that you have a record of the codes.

Now that we have decided upon our variable names and codes for categorical data, as illustrated in Figure 2.1, we can set up the SPSS database.

2.3 Setting up an SPSS database

When you open SPSS you should be faced with the following screen:

Screenshot 2.1

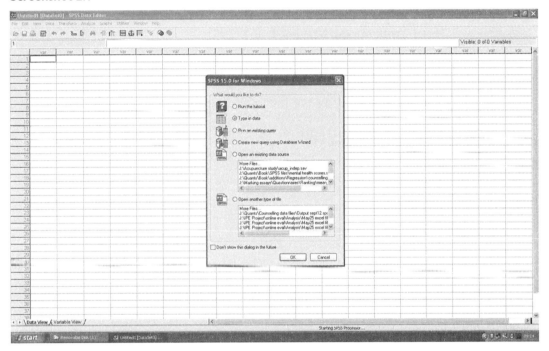

Click **Type in data** and then click **OK**. This opens a blank spreadsheet.

The SPSS data screen

The screen below is known as the **Data View**. This is where you will enter the data. *But not yet – there's a little more reading to do.*

Each *row* will contain the data for one patient. So, in the example on the next page, we have data for 3 patients:

- Patient 1 is a male (coded 1), aged 24.
- Patient 2 is a female (coded 2), aged 25.
- Patient 3 is male, aged 26.

Screenshot 2.2

2.3.1 Defining the variables

Before we can enter our data, we need to enter variable names and coding instructions.

On the bottom left of the Data Editor screen you will see two *tabs* labelled **Data View** and **Variable View**.

Screenshot 2.3

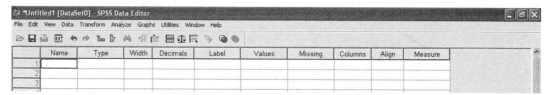

Click on **Variable View**. This will produce the following screen where you will type in information about the variables:

Screenshot 2.4

In this view each *row* will provide information for each variable. This is where we need to refer to our SPSS codebook (see Figure 2.1).

Name

Enter the first SPSS variable name listed in your codebook, i.e., **patient**. Then press the right arrow on your keyboard to go to the next column – *type*.

Box 2.1 SPSS rules for naming variables

SPSS has a number of rules for naming variables:

- The length of the name cannot exceed 64 characters. Though, clearly, you should keep the variable name as short and succinct as possible, as we have done for the counselling questionnaire.
- The name must begin with a letter. The remaining characters can be any letter, any digit, a full stop or the symbols @, #, _ or $.
- Variable names cannot contain spaces or end with a full stop.
- Each variable name must be unique: duplication is not allowed.
- Reserved keywords cannot be used as variable names. Reserved keywords are: ALL, AND, BY, EQ, GE, GT, LE, LT, NE, NOT, OR, TO, WITH.
- Variable names can be defined with any mixture of upper and lower case characters.

Type: what type of data is it?

Once you have entered a variable name the default value for **Type** will appear automatically as numeric. All of our variables will be numeric because we will be coding any words – such as male and female – as numbers (i.e., 1 for male and 2 for female). So you can move on to the next column – **Width** (see Box 2.2 for occasions when you really have to enter words).

Box 2.2 Entering words into SPSS

There are certain occasions when you might want to enter words into SPSS. For example, if the data forms part of a database where you need to retain the names of individuals. Or it may be that you are copying data into SPSS, from an Excel spreadsheet, for example, which includes words. If you do not tell SPSS to expect words it may not recognize them (your column of words from Excel may not appear).

As an example, if we wanted to enter the words 'male' and 'female' (instead of numbers) we would need to click in the cell and a shaded square with three dots will appear. Click on this and a list of options will appear:

Screenshot 2.5

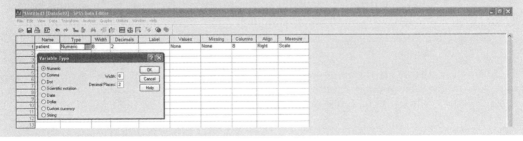

In SPSS words are known as string variables. So, we would click on **String** and then **OK** and this cell would say **String**, rather than **Numeric**. Notice also that SPSS provides options to enter dates or currency data.

Width: how many numbers will you be entering?

SPSS defaults to eight characters. The most we will need is two – for our age and session data (e.g., 24 years, 12 sessions). There is no need to change this. You would increase it if you were entering very large numbers, for example, 184,333,333.24 (i.e., 11 numbers/characters).

Decimals

SPSS defaults to two decimal places. Since our data does not require decimal places we can simply click in the **Decimals** cell and click the up or down arrows (which appear to the right of the cell) to adjust decimal places needed for that particular variable.

Screenshot 2.6

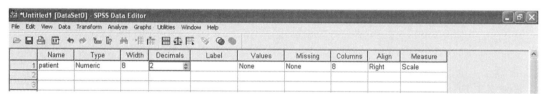

For datasets with many variables that do not have decimal places it may be worthwhile changing the default setting to 0 decimal places. You can do this by clicking on **Edit** from the menu at the top of the screen and then choosing **Options**. Next, click the **Data** tab and change the decimal place value to 0 in **Display** format for new numeric variables.

Label

The **Label** column allows you to provide a longer description of your variable, which will be shown in the output produced by SPSS. You do not need to put anything here for 'patient', or the other variables, since the names are self-explanatory.[2]

Values

Values are numbers assigned to categories for nominal variables, for example, where male = 1 and female = 2. Since your first variable (patient) has no 'values', you do not need to put anything here.

Missing

Sometimes it is useful to assign specific values to indicate different reasons for missing data. However, SPSS recognizes any blank cell as missing data and excludes it from any calculations, so if you intend to leave the cell blank there is no need to enter values for missing data. And we have no missing data anyway.[3]

Columns

You can change the column width to reduce the space it takes on the screen. But you need to allow enough space for variable names, so the default of eight is usually OK.

Align

This is usually set at **Right**, which is OK.

Measure

The default measure is **Scale**, but you can change this to **Ordinal** or **Nominal** by clicking in the cell and then on the down arrow on the right of the cell. We have scale data and nominal data:

Table 2.2 Measure definitions

Measure	Definition
Scale:	For numeric values on an interval or ratio scale: age, sessions, satisfaction.
Nominal:	For values that represent categories with no intrinsic order: patient, sex, counsellor.
Ordinal:	For values with some intrinsic order (e.g., low, medium, high; first, second third).

Since our first variable is simply listing the patient/questionnaire number we should change this to 'nominal' because the numbers are simply assigned to the patients (they have no meaning as a scale).

You should now have completed the information for the first variable, 'patient', and it should look like this:

Screenshot 2.7

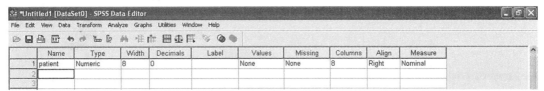

2.3.2. Adding value labels

The next variable is 'sex'. Proceed as you did for 'patient' until you get to **Values**. Whereas 'patient' had no values – it was simply patient numbers – sex has two values: we will be entering the number 1 for male and number 2 for female. So you need to tell SPSS that is what you are doing.

This is how you add value labels in SPSS:

1 Click in the **Values** cell and then on the button with 3 dots on the right side of the cell. This opens the **Value Label** box.
2 Click in the box marked **Value**. Type in 1.
3 Click in the box marked **Value Label**. Type in male.
4 Click on **Add**. You will then see in the summary box: 1=male.
5 Repeat this procedure for females (**Value** = 2; **Value Label**: female; **Add**).

Screenshot 2.8

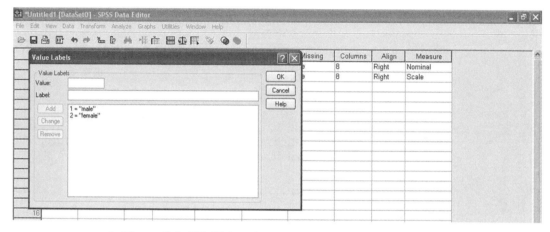

6 Then click **OK**. This information is now stored in your SPSS database. The only other thing to change is **Measure** (to **Nominal**) and your database should look like this:

Screenshot 2.9

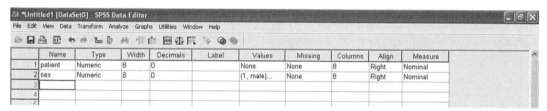

7 You should now be able to complete the information for the remaining variables, ensuring that you enter the value labels for 'counsellor' (1 = John; 2 = Jane).

When you have done this your database should look like this:

Screenshot 2.10

	Name	Type	Width	Decimals	Label	Values	Missing	Columns	Align	Measure
1	patient	Numeric	8	0		None	None	8	Right	Nominal
2	sex	Numeric	8	0		{1, male}...	None	8	Right	Nominal
3	age	Numeric	8	0		None	None	8	Right	Scale
4	counsellor	Numeric	8	0		{1, John}...	None	8	Right	Nominal
5	sessions	Numeric	8	0		None	None	8	Right	Scale
6	satisfaction	Numeric	8	0		None	None	8	Right	Scale
7										
8										

You have now defined your variables and can proceed to enter the data.

2.4 Entering the data

Click the **Data View** tab (bottom left of screen) and this will switch you from **Variable View** to **Data View**. Notice that the columns are now headed with your variable names.

Screenshot 2.11

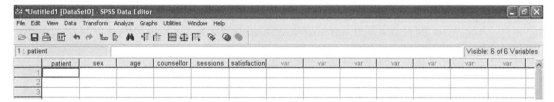

You can now enter the data for the 30 patients. Simply click in the top left-hand cell (patient 1) and enter 1. Then move to the next cell (press the right arrow on your keyboard) and enter the data for each patient according to the data in Table 2.1. This should result in the following data:

Screenshot 2.12

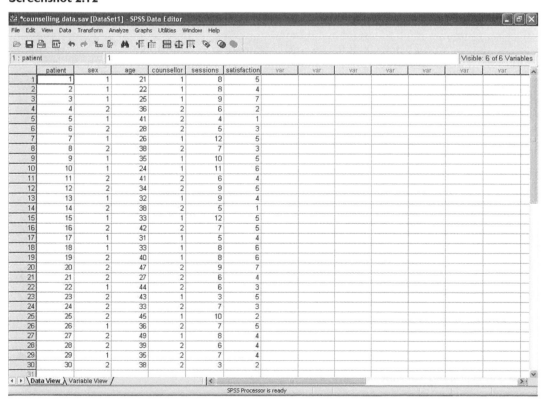

Once you have entered the data make sure you save the file.[4]

We are now ready to begin the analyses. That is, after you have done the following exercises.

2.5 Exercises

Exercise 2.1 Viewing value labels

In order to check that you have entered the data correctly you might wish to display your value labels so that the SPSS dataset looks exactly like the data in Table 2.1. You can view the value labels by clicking **View**, then click **Value Labels**:

Screenshot 2.13

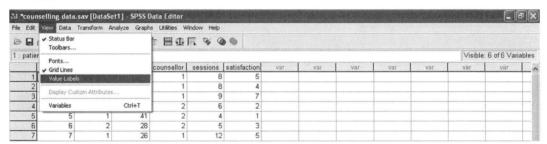

Your value labels for sex and counsellor are now displayed:

Screenshot 2.14

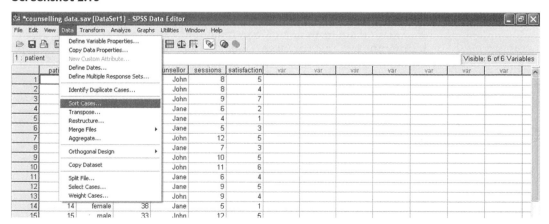

Exercise 2.2　Sorting the data

Sometimes it is useful to re-order the data, for example, if you wanted to visually examine all the male cases together.[5] To do this:

1 From the menu at the top of the screen, click **Data**, then click **Sort Cases**.

Screenshot 2.15

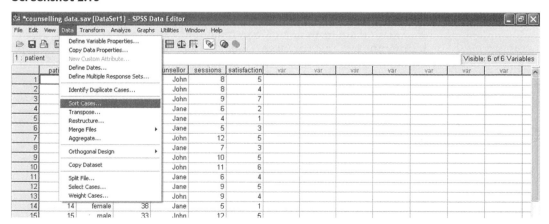

2 Click on the variable **sex**, then click the arrow (to the left of the Sort by box) to move it into the **Sort by** box:

Screenshot 2.16

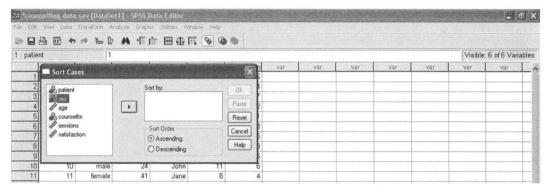

3 You can now click **OK** to sort your dataset by the sex of the patient:

Screenshot 2.17

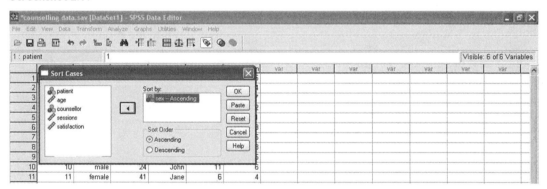

4 Your dataset is now re-ordered with all the male patients at the top (see Screenshot 2.18).

Note: If you are working in SPSS v15 an **Output Viewer** screen will appear logging the fact that you have conducted a procedure in SPSS. Close this by clicking the cross in the orange box to the top right of the **Output Viewer** screen. When it asks if you want to save this, click **no**.

Screenshot 2.18

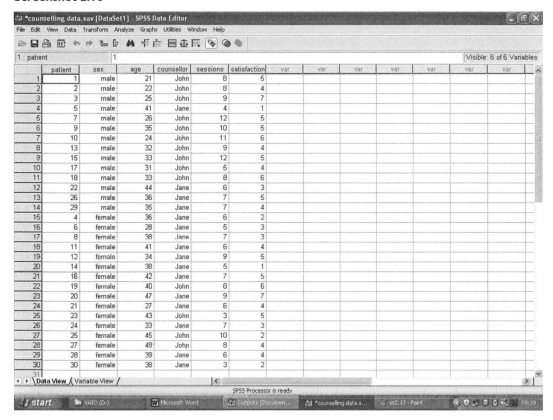

5 To get the data back into its original order, go back to **Data/Sort Cases**. Double-click (left mouse button) on **Patient** to sort the data back into its original order. (And note that we would not have been able to do this if we had not numbered each patient/questionnaire.)

You can actually sort by as many variables as you want – at the same time. For example, you could sort the data by **sex** of patients *and* **age** by putting both variables in the Sort by box, but really, I think we need to get on with the analysis.

Notes

1 This is an arbitrary assignment of the numbers 1 and 2, and is not meant in any way to reflect the order of importance of the male and female genders. I point this out because one student did raise this issue (in class) and it was debated for some time. . .

2 You might make use of the **Label** facility if you had a long questionnaire and you decided to label your variables q1, q2, q3, etc. In the **Label** column you would provide a description of each particular question. For example, if we took this approach for the counselling questionnaire, the label for q4

would be 'number of counselling sessions' – and this label would appear in the output rather than 'q4' to help us identify the particular question. This approach used to be more common in older versions of SPSS when we were limited to eight characters in the variable column, so truncated (barely identifiable) names often needed to be entered.

3   As an example, we might want to differentiate missing data due to a patient refusing to answer a sensitive question, and missing data due to a question not being applicable to a patient. In such cases we would need to click in the **Missing** cell whereupon a button with three dots will appear to the right of the cell; a dialogue box then appears where you can enter a value for the missing data. The value you enter should be out of the range of values that may occur as part of the data: 99 is a commonly used value to define missing data – though if your variable may legitimately include that value (potentially 'age' in our dataset) you should choose a more remote number (999).

4   And make sure you know *where* you have saved it! There have been a few occasions when students have saved the data file on the university network but were unable to locate it for the next session. Also, if you *are* working on a university or college computer you should also be aware that some computers are programmed to 'log out' after a specified period if they are not being used; if you leave the computer without saving the file, the data may not be there when you return . . .

5   Sorting the data can be useful for a number of reasons. I recently found it useful for a questionnaire where I needed to edit the dataset according to the month patients were referred to a service. Sorting the cases according to month of referral made this much easier.

3 | Descriptive statistics: frequencies, measures of central tendency and illustrating the data using graphs

In this chapter you will use SPSS to produce some basic descriptive statistics from the data: frequencies for categorical data and measures of central tendency for interval level data. You will also learn how to produce and edit charts to illustrate the data analysis, and how to copy your work into a Microsoft Word file.

3.1 Frequencies

We noted in Chapter 1 that the first thing a researcher would do with this data is to 'run some frequencies'. This simply means that we want to look at the frequencies of our *categorical* data:

- How many male/female patients are there?
- How many patients were treated by each of the counsellors John and Jane?

This will provide us with an initial overview of our sample, or 'population'.

So let us start with our first categorical variable – sex.

Running frequencies in SPSS

1 From the menu at the top of the screen click **Analyze**, then **Descriptive Statistics** then **Frequencies**.

Screenshot 3.1

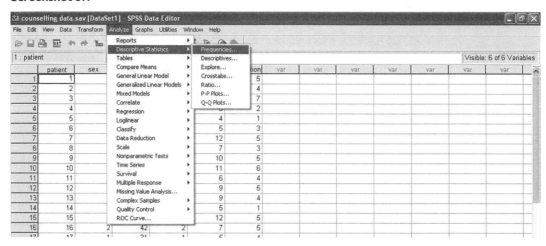

2 Choose the variable **sex** by clicking with your mouse.
3 Once **sex** is highlighted move it across into the variables box by clicking the
   arrow. Alternatively you could just double-click it once it is highlighted.

Screenshot 3.2

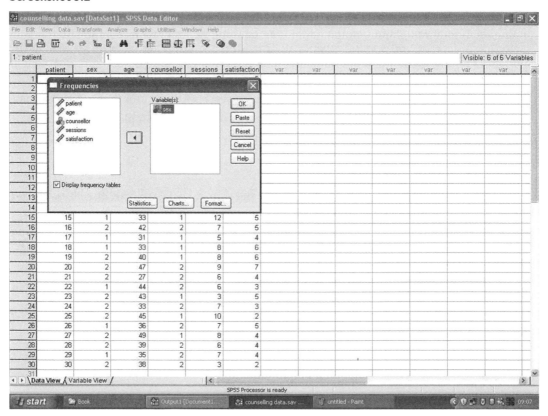

4 Now click **OK**.

A new SPSS window should now appear. This is called the **Output Viewer**, as shown next. The results of all analyses performed by SPSS will appear in this viewer – which can be saved separately as a file.

Note: You may need to maximize this screen by clicking the maximize button (top right of screen – middle icon to the left of the x).

Screenshot 3.3

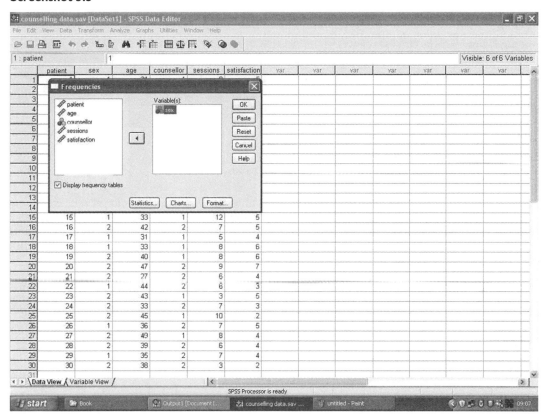

This has produced the frequencies analysis for the variable sex in the form of an SPSS 'pivot table'. The first column has the labels male and female in it: if you had not entered value labels, instead of male there would be a 1, and instead of female there would be a 2. The second column tells us that there are 30 cases: 14 are male and 16 are female. The third column provides percentages.

The fourth column – **Valid Percent** – calculates percentage *ignoring any missing values*. Since there are no missing values here, valid per cent is the same as actual per cent. But in the hypothetical example on the next page, I have removed data for ten cases.

Screenshot 3.4

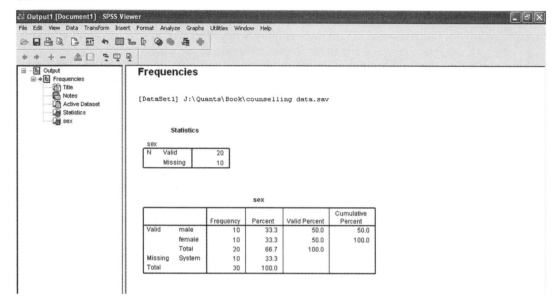

When we have missing data the values for *per cent* and *valid per cent* are different. This is because the per cent column calculates percentages for all the data – including missing data. So, in the output above, we have ten males, ten females and ten missing data – each of which constitutes 33.3 per cent of the total data – 30 cases.

Valid per cent, however, ignores the missing data (ten cases) and has calculated percentage based on a total of 20 cases. Thus, 20/10 = 50%. *If you have missing data this is the percentage figure you should cite.*

Note that you now have two SPSS windows in operation:

- SPSS **Data Editor** (with data and variable views).
- **Output Viewer.**

You can switch between the two by clicking the tabs at the bottom of your screen.

Screenshot 3.5

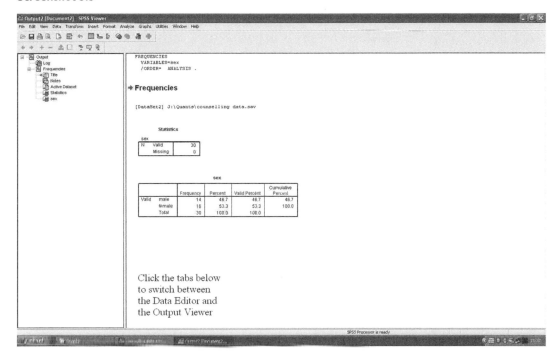

Now try running frequencies for the other categorical variable – **counsellor** – to see how many patients they each treated.

Go to the menu at the top of the screen and click **Analyze** then **Descriptive Statistics** then **Frequencies**. You should then remove the variable **sex** from the frequencies analysis box by double-clicking it with the left mouse button. You can now run frequencies for **counsellor**, which should result in the following output:

Screenshot 3.6

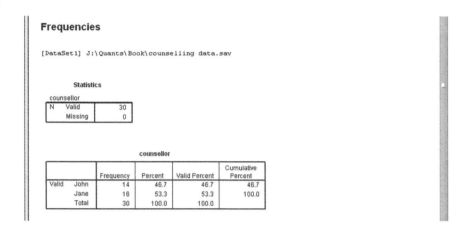

Frequencies

[DataSet1] J:\Quants\Book\counselling data.sav

Statistics

counsellor

N	Valid	30
	Missing	0

counsellor

		Frequency	Percent	Valid Percent	Cumulative Percent
Valid	John	14	46.7	46.7	46.7
	Jane	16	53.3	53.3	100.0
	Total	30	100.0	100.0	

You can in fact run **Frequencies** for more than one variable at a time by moving them all into the **Variables** box, as shown below:

Screenshot 3.7

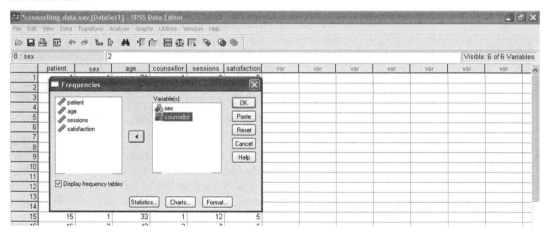

3.2 Measures of central tendency for interval variables

Having examined frequencies for our categorical data, we now need to examine our variables containing interval data: age, number of sessions and satisfaction with the service.

Our aim here is to obtain basic, descriptive information about these variables. For example, we should want to know the age range of patients attending for counselling and the mean (or median) age of our sample. This is basic information that the doctor would want to know about the 'population' attending for counselling. So, the information we are seeking is:

1 What is the mean/median:

- age of patients;
- number of sessions;
- satisfaction rating.

2 What is the range of values – from lowest to highest – for:

- age of patients;
- number of sessions;
- satisfaction ratings.

We can obtain this information by running **Frequencies** for age, sessions and satisfaction.

Running frequencies for measures of central tendency

1 From the menu at the top of the screen click **Analyze**, then **Descriptive Statistics**, then **Frequencies** (remove any existing variables from previous analyses by double-clicking them to return them to the list).
2 Double-click (left mouse button) the variables **age**, **sessions** and **satisfaction** to move them into the **Variables** box.
3 Click **Statistics** and click in the boxes next to mean, median, mode, and minimum and maximum. Then click **Continue**.

Screenshot 3.8

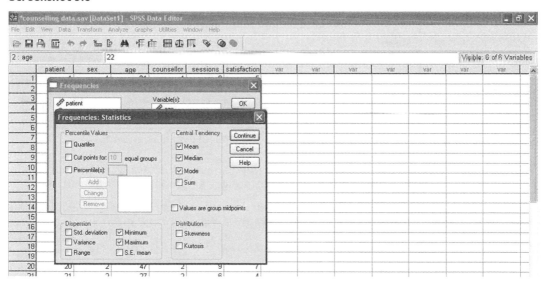

4 De-select **Display Frequency Tables** (otherwise you will get a table listing every age).

Screenshot 3.9

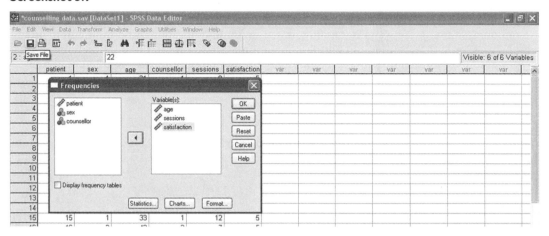

5   Click OK, and this should produce the output table below:

Table 3.1 SPSS descriptive statistics

Statistics

		age	sessions	satisfaction
N	Valid	30	30	30
	Missing	0	0	0
Mean		35.20	7.37	4.13
Median		35.50	7.00	4.00
Mode		33ª	6ª	4ª
Minimum		21	3	1
Maximum		49	12	7

a. Multiple modes exist. The smallest value is shown

This table provides us with information about the mean, median and mode, and the lowest and highest values (range of scores) for our three variables.

Focusing on the variable 'age', we can see that mean age was 35.2 years and the median age was 35.5 years. Since these values for the mean and the median are very similar this tells us that our data is not skewed towards one end of the scale (as we discussed in detail in Chapter 1). We can also see that ages ranged from 21 years to 49 years.

The modal age (most common actual age) is also provided (33 years), but note that SPSS tells us that 'multiple modes exist' and that this is the smallest value. The most commonly occurring age is not, of course, very useful for our data analysis.

The modal value may, however, be of more interest for the other two variables. So while we know that the mean number of sessions is 7, it may also be interesting to know that the modal number of sessions was actually 6 if the doctor or counselling service is recommending that most patients should be limited to 6 sessions. Similarly, although we know that the mean satisfaction rating is a relatively neutral 4, it may be useful to know that the modal rating is also 4. The mean value of 4 could have come from data that was an average of very low and very high ratings – indicating that patients were divided in their perceptions of the service; a modal rating of 4 suggests that this is not the case (though note of course that SPSS tells us that multiple modes exist).

So, in our report to the doctor, from the analyses we have so far conducted, we can inform him about:

- The frequencies or number of patients seen by each of the counsellors, and their gender.
- The mean/median age, number of sessions and satisfaction rating, along with the range of values for each of these variables.

This information would be an important first step in presenting the results of our analysis to the doctor.

3.3 Using graphs to visually illustrate the data

This information may also be graphically illustrated using bar charts, histograms and boxplots.

3.3.1 Bar charts

Bar charts present a graphical display of categorical data, for example, comparing the mean number of sessions provided by each counsellor.

Producing a bar chart comparing the mean number of sessions provided by each counsellor

1 From the menu at the top of the screen click **Graphs**, then **Chart Builder** (a dialogue box may appear asking if you have set the correct measurement levels for each variable and included value labels for categorical variables). Since you have done both (you have, haven't you . . .), put a tick next to **Do not show this dialogue again** and click **OK**).
2 You should then be faced with the following screen:

Screenshot 3.10

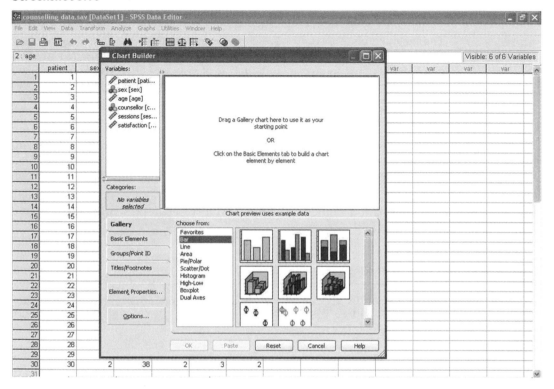

3 In the **Gallery** of charts, **Bar** should be highlighted showing a range of
   bar charts (simple, clustered, stacked). Since we want to produce a simple
   bar chart, click (left mouse button) on the first **Bar Chart** (top left) and drag
   it into the **Preview** area above. A bar chart will now appear in the preview
   area with two boxes asking for the Y-axis and the X-axis.

Screenshot 3.11

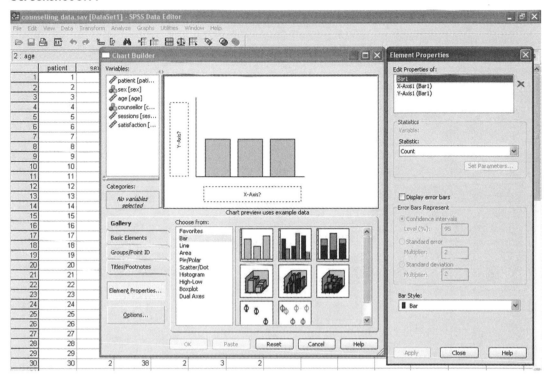

4 Drag **counsellor** from the **Variables** list into the X-axis and then drag
   sessions into the Y-axis.

Screenshot 3.12

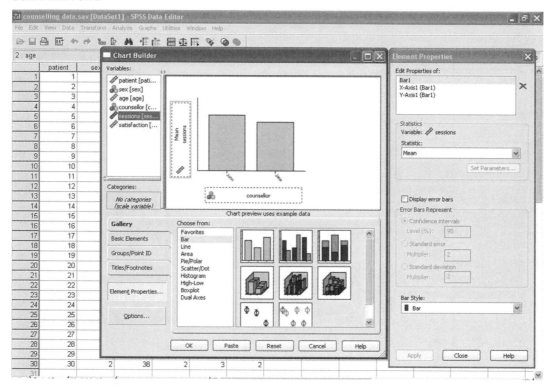

5 Click **OK** and this will produce the following bar chart in the output
   viewer:

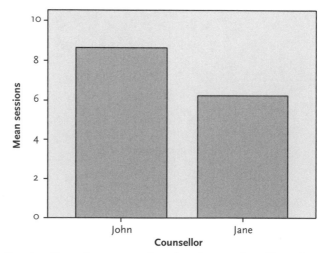

Figure 3.1 Bar chart illustrating mean number of sessions conducted by each counsellor

From the bar chart we can see that Jane has kept to the guidelines of providing an average of six sessions of 'brief therapy' compared to John who has been providing an average of over eight sessions.

3.3.2 Histograms

Histograms are similar to bar charts but are designed to represent data along a continuum. The age of patients is a good example.

Using SPSS to produce a histogram for age

1 From the menu at the top of the screen click **Graphs**, then **Chart Builder**.
2 Select **Histogram** from the Gallery of Charts to reveal the range of charts available.
3 Drag the first histogram (top left) into the preview area.
4 From the variables list drag **age** into the X-axis.

Screenshot 3.13

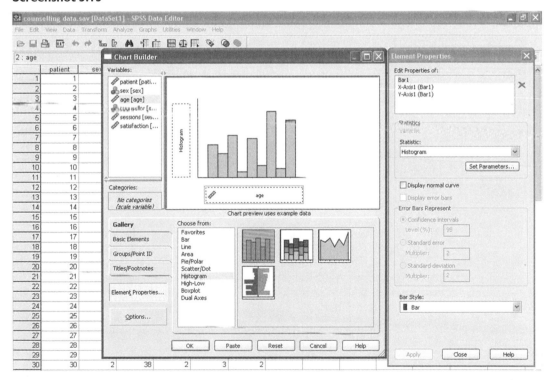

5 Click **OK** and this should produce the following histogram in the output viewer:

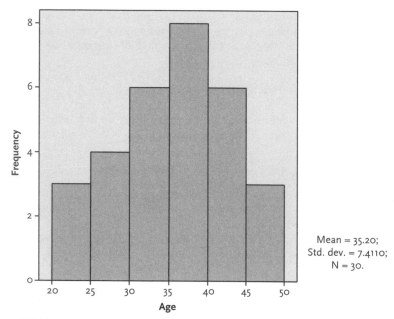

Figure 3.2 Histogram showing age distribution of patients

From the histogram we can see that the age of patients is 'normally distributed' with the majority in the age range 30 years to 45 years, tailing off at the younger and older ages.

Note: the bars in the histogram are not separated by gaps – because they represent data along a continuum – unlike the bars in the bar chart which represent discrete categories.

3.3.3 Editing a chart

You may want to edit the histogram for age. For example, you might want to edit the labels for the X- (horizontal) and Y- (vertical) axis: perhaps 'frequency' should be changed to 'number'; and you might also want to add that age is in years. Also, to the right-hand side of the graph there is information about the mean, standard deviation (discussed later) and number of students, that you might want to remove.

To edit a chart you need to double-click it with your left mouse button. This will open the **Chart Editor**.

Screenshot 3.14

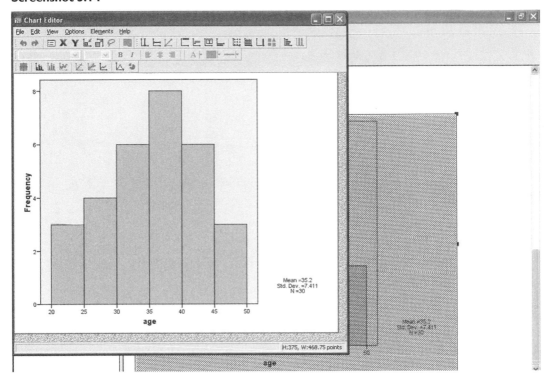

There are various changes you can make once the Chart Editor is open, and really you need to find out by trial and error – mainly by highlighting the bits you want to change by clicking or double-clicking with the left mouse button.

For example, in order to delete the information on the right of the chart, I clicked the left mouse button once over this information, then I clicked the right mouse button to produce the menu shown in Screenshot 3.15. I then moved down to **Delete** to remove this information. (A 'Properties' box appears in SPSS v15 informing you that the chart will be resized when elements are added or removed – uncheck the box next to 'Resize elements . . .' and click **Apply** then **Close** if you want the graph to remain the same size (or leave it ticked if your prefer a wider graph).

Screenshot 3.15

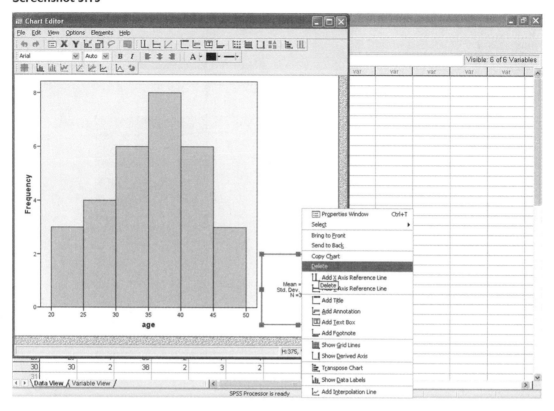

To edit the labels 'age' and 'frequency' click on them once with the left mouse button to highlight them, and then click again (left mouse button) to produce a flashing cursor; you can then re-write your own labels in the text box.

Screenshot 3.16

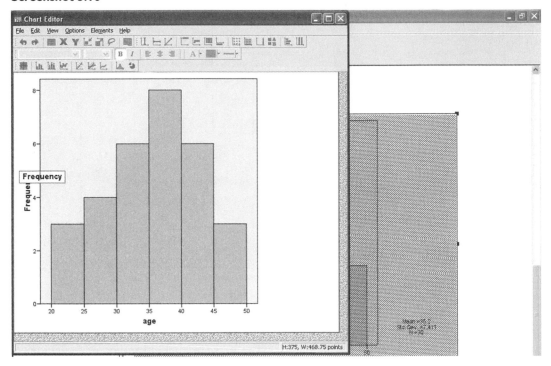

Finally, I produced the following version of the histogram – having edited the labels and removed the data to the right of the chart. Presentation is very important for reports, so attention to details like this, rather than just accepting what is produced by SPSS, can make a significant difference to the quality of a report.

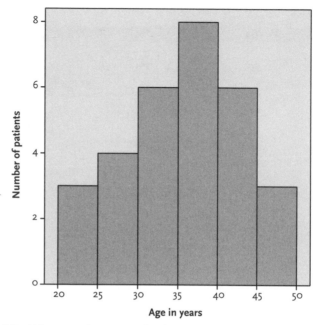

Figure 3.3 Edited histogram showing age distribution of patients

There are numerous changes you can make by clicking and double-clicking on the bits of the chart you are interesting in changing and you should simply try them out yourself.

3.3.4 Boxplots

Another useful way to illustrate the spread of the data is to use boxplots.

Using SPSS to produce boxplots for age and gender

1 From the menu at the top of the screen click **Graphs**, then **Chart Builder**.
2 Select **Boxplot** from the **Gallery of Charts** to reveal the range of boxplot charts available.
3 Drag the first boxplot (simple boxplot) into the preview area.
4 From the variables list drag **age** into the Y-axis and **sex** into the X-axis.
5 Click **OK**.

This should produce the following output: two boxplots illustrating the distribution of age for male and females in the sample.

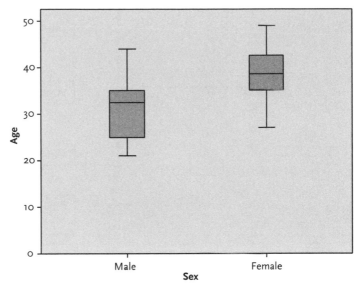

Figure 3.4 Boxplots illustrating age distribution of male and female patients

These boxplots illustrate the spread of the data:

- the shaded box contains the middle 50 per cent of values;
- the line inside the box depicts the median value (*not the mean*);
- the T-bar lines above and below the box reach to the highest and lowest values.

So, from these boxplots comparing the ages of our males and females, we can see that the median age of females is higher and, overall, the age ranges are higher. The spread of ages, indicated by the size of the shaded boxes and the length of the T-bars, is roughly similar for both groups.

Figure 3.5 provides a detailed description of the information provided in box-plots. Notice the added inclusion of 'outliers' and 'extreme cases' which often occur in large datasets. For example, if 29 patients attended for between four and eight counselling sessions and one attended for 12 sessions this might be considered an 'outlier' or, more severely, an 'extreme value' because it deviates from the norm.

These cases deserve special attention since they may skew any measures of central tendency. For example, a couple of extremely high ages would have increased the mean value, leaving the median the same. Outliers and extreme cases may also, of course, simply indicate an error in data entry which often occurs in large datasets.

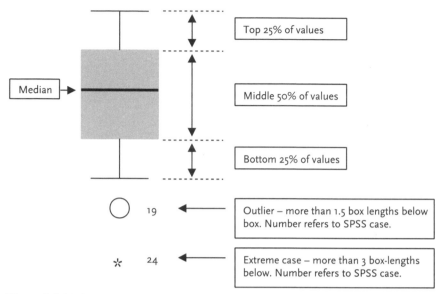

Figure 3.5 Understanding boxplots

3.3.5 Copying charts and tables into a Microsoft Word document

If you are producing a report of your data analysis it will often be useful to copy the output from SPSS into a Microsoft Word document.

For charts, like the boxplot above, you should first double-click the object to open the **Chart Editor**. Then, from the menu at the top of the screen click **Edit** and **Copy Chart**.

Screenshot 3.17

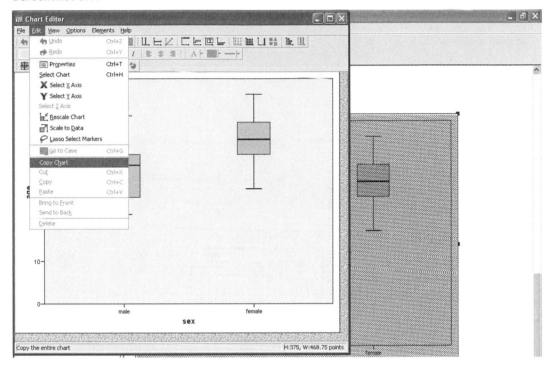

You can then paste the chart into a Microsoft Word document (obviously, you will first need to open a Word document).[1]

You can copy tables from the SPSS output file into a Word file by highlighting the table (click left mouse button over **Table**), then click the right mouse button on **Copy Objects**, and paste into the Word document.

Screenshot 3.18

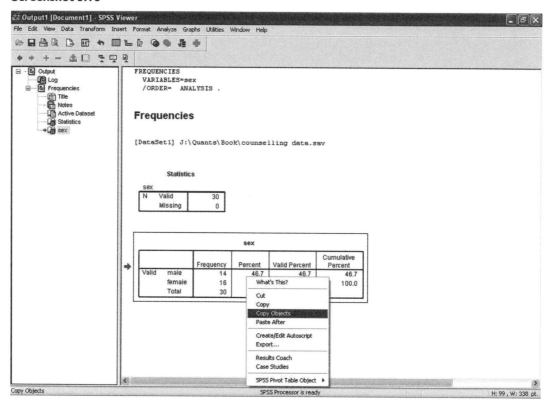

In the example above I chose the option **Copy Objects** rather than **Copy**. If you copy the table as an object you will not be able to edit the table when it is in the Microsoft Word document:

Screenshot 3.19

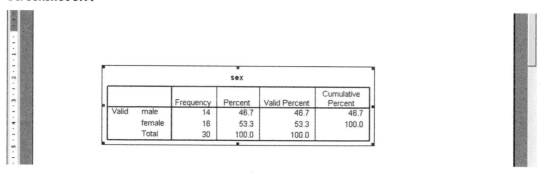

If you do want to edit a table you should choose **Copy**:

Screenshot 3.20

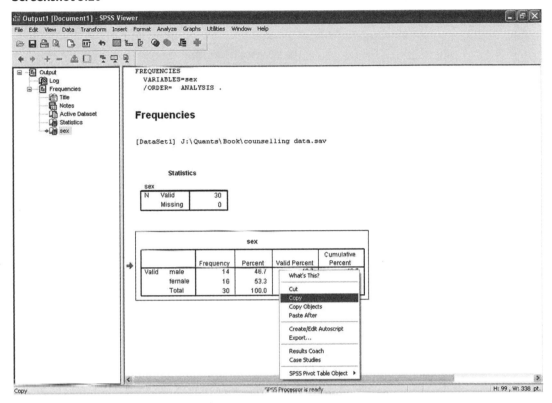

When you paste it into a Microsoft Word document you will then be able to edit the table. For example, you might want to remove the last two columns since they do not provide useful information on this occasion. To do this, highlight the last two columns and click the right mouse button:

Screenshot 3.21

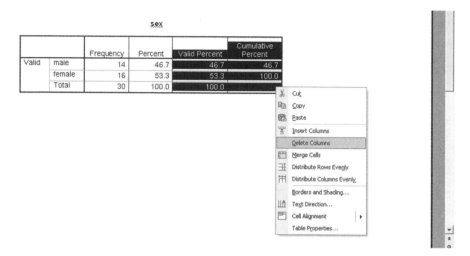

When you press Delete Columns you will be left with a table that has no irrelevant information, which may confuse the reader:

Table 3.2 The edited table

		Frequency	Percent
Valid	male	14	46.7
	female	16	53.3
	Total	30	100.0

3.3.6 Navigating the Output Viewer

You will now have amassed a considerable number of analyses in your **Output Viewer**. Sometimes it is useful to tidy up at this stage, perhaps removing any output analyses that you no longer need. To do this click in the left-hand pane listing the output to remove any analyses that you do not want to keep.

Screenshot 3.22

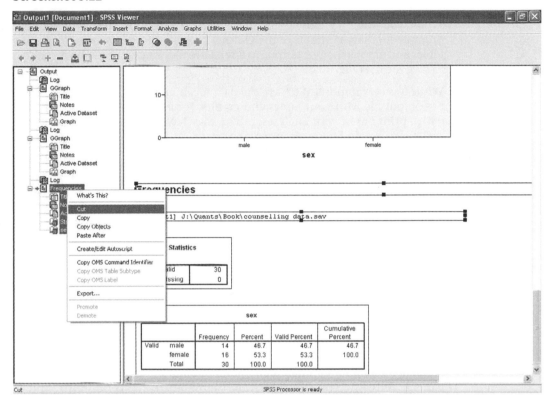

3.4 Summary

In this chapter you have learnt:

- How to produce frequencies for categorical data.
- When you should refer to the 'valid per cent' rather than overall per cent, i.e., when there is missing data.
- How to produce measures of central tendency (means, medians and modes), and minimum and maximum values, for interval data.
- How to produce bar charts, histograms and boxplots to visually illustrate the data.
- How to copy your SPSS output into a Microsoft Word document.
- How to navigate the SPSS Output Viewer.

You now have the skills to enter data into SPSS, code it, and produce basic descriptive statistics for categorical and interval data.

3.5 Ending the SPSS session

When you want to close SPSS simply go to **File/Exit**. You will then be prompted to 'save contents of the Output Viewer'. This allows you to save the tables and graphs in your output to a separate file. You will then be prompted to save the data file.

While it is very important to save the data file, it may be less important to save the output file with your tables and graphs. For example, you may be happy with a print out of your analyses, or you may have copied the relevant tables and charts into a Microsoft Word document. As long as you have saved the data file, it may be relatively simple to run the analyses again – depending on how much you have done of course.

3.6 Exercises

Exercise 3.1

You have already produced a histogram for the variable age. Now produce histograms illustrating the distribution of sessions and satisfaction ratings. What sort of distribution do they display? Is the data 'normally distributed'?

Exercise 3.2

Produce boxplots comparing satisfaction ratings according to the gender of patients. What do you conclude from the results in terms of: (a) the spread of the data for males compared to females; (b) the relative satisfaction ratings of males compared to females?

Are you happy with the chart or do you need to use Chart Editor?

Exercise 3.3

There is a facility in SPSS that allows you to change the way your data and outputs, (such as charts and tables) are displayed. One particularly relevant option enables you to change the way tables are displayed in SPSS output. For example, if you are intending to submit your report for publication in a journal you may actually need to change the way your tables are displayed in accordance with the journal guidelines.

In order to change the settings for tables, click on **Edit** from the menu at the top of the screen and then choose **Options**. You should then be presented with the following table on your screen:

Screenshot 3.23

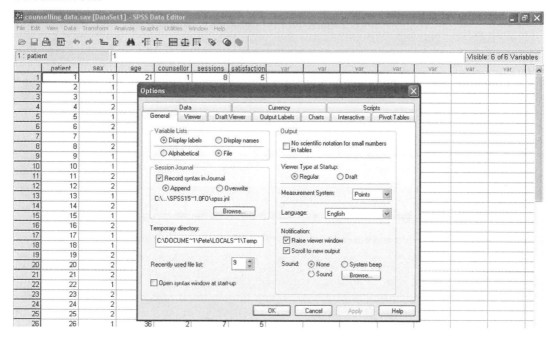

If you click on the **Pivot Tables** tab you can choose the format of your tables. Clicking on the **Table look** provides a preview or sample of how the tables will look. The three tables below are provided as examples:

Table 3.3 System default table: sex

SEX

		Frequency	Percent	Valid Percent	Cumulative Percent
Valid	male	820	38.8	38.8	38.8
	female	1295	61.2	61.2	100.0
	Total	2115	100.0	100.0	

You might want to choose **smallfont.tlo** to save paper when printing out results of many analyses.

Table 3.4 Smallfont.tlo: paper-saving table (sex)

SEX

		Frequency	Percent	Valid Percent	Cumulative Percent
Valid	male	820	38.8	38.8	38.8
	female	1295	61.2	61.2	100.0
	Total	2115	100.0	100.0	

Many journals use APA (American Psychological Association) style which does not use vertical lines. So, if you want to import a table from SPSS into a file you are submitting to a journal, you might use one of the academic formats as in Table 3.5.

Table 3.5 academic style table (sex)

SEX

		Frequency	Percent	Valid Percent	Cumulative Percent
Valid	male	820	38.8	38.8	38.8
	female	1295	61.2	61.2	100.0
	Total	2115	100.0	100.0	

Note: You have to change the style *before* you run the analyses.

3.7 Notes

1 Alternatively, you can simply use the right mouse button to copy the chart straight from the output viewer without going into Chart Editor. However, I find that this leaves a larger frame around the chart taking up more space in the Microsoft Word document. Try it and see for yourself.

4 Cross-tabulation and the chi-square statistic

In this chapter you will learn about cross-tabulation for categorical data, a statistical test (chi-square) to examine associations between variables and the concept of statistical significance. You will also learn how to re-code interval data into categories.

4.1 Introduction

Cross-tabulation is one of the most frequently used methods of analysis for questionnaire data. It enables us to examine the relationship between categorical variables in greater detail than simple frequencies for individual variables. In this chapter we will see how to do this in SPSS and also apply a statistical analysis associated with cross-tabulation – known as chi-square (pronounced 'kye square').

4.2 Cross-tabulating data in the questionnaire

In our counselling satisfaction questionnaire we have only two categorical variables: sex of the patient (male or female), and counsellor (John or Jane). When we ran frequencies for these two variables in the previous chapter we obtained the following results:

Table 4.1 Number of male and female patients

sex

		Frequency	Percent	Valid Percent	Cumulative Percent
Valid	male	14	46.7	46.7	46.7
	female	16	53.3	53.3	100.0
	Total	30	100.0	100.0	

Table 4.2 Number of patients seen by each counsellor

counsellor

		Frequency	Percent	Valid Percent	Cumulative Percent
Valid	John	14	46.7	46.7	46.7
	Jane	16	53.3	53.3	100.0
	Total	30	100.0	100.0	

From these frequency tables we could see that the number of male and female patients was quite evenly distributed (14 male, 16 female) and that the counsellors each saw a similar number of patients (John saw 14, Jane saw 16).

But what about the relationship between these two variables? That is, did each of the counsellors see a similar number of male and female patients or were they quite different proportions? To find out we need to run a cross-tabulation in SPSS.

Running cross-tabulations in SPSS

1 From the menu at the top of the screen click **Analyze** then **Descriptive Statistics** then **Crosstabs**.
2 Move the variable **sex** into the rows box and **counsellor** into the columns box.
3 Click the **Cells** button. In this box the observed counts should already be ticked (this simply provides the observed frequencies). You should also click **Row percentages** – since we want to know the percentages of males and females who were treated by each counsellor.

Screenshot 4.1

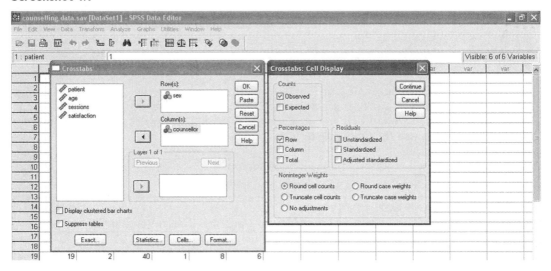

4 Click **Continue** to close this box, and then click **OK** to run the analysis.

This should produce the following table in your output viewer.

Table 4.3 Cross-tabulation of sex and counsellor

sex * counsellor Crosstabulation

			counsellor		
			John	Jane	Total
sex	male	Count	10	4	14
		% within sex	71.4%	28.6%	100.0%
	female	Count	4	12	16
		% within sex	25.0%	75.0%	100.0%
Total		Count	14	16	30
		% within sex	46.7%	53.3%	100.0%

From this table we can see the numbers and relative percentages of males and females who were treated by each counsellor. In particular, we can see that while the majority (71%) of male patients saw John, the majority of female patients (75%) saw Jane. Clearly then, the proportion of male/female patients were not equally distributed across the two counsellors: the female counsellor tended to see female patients, and the male counsellor tended to see male patients. This might suggest a preference among patients to see a same-sex counsellor to discuss their problems. We noted in the overview from Chapter 1 that this might be important information for the doctor and should be included in any report, since this might suggest it is necessary to ensure a male and a female counsellor are available to cater for patient preferences.[1]

4.3 The chi-square statistical test

We have seen, then, that the sex of patients was not equally distributed across the counsellors. But we might ask was this a chance result? If we started the service again and the patients were *randomly* assigned to the counsellors might we have found a similar result? Perhaps even the opposite – with most male patients seeing the female counsellor. More likely of course, by chance, we would expect them to be distributed quite evenly across the sexes. The question is: how much of an unequal distribution across the sexes does there have to be for us to conclude that there was a significant bias for male patients to see a male counsellor and vice versa? Or, to put it another way: how much of an unequal distribution across the sexes does there have to be for us to *reject the possibility that this has occurred by chance*? This is where a statistical test comes in handy.

Chi-square (represented as χ^2) applies a statistical test to cross-tabulation by comparing the actual *observed* frequencies in each cell of tables with *expected* frequencies. Expected frequencies are those we would expect if data is 'randomly distributed'.

It may help at this point to think of the four cells in the cross-tabulation table as buckets. Now imagine a lottery machine designed to pump balls into each of the buckets through four pipes – one leading into each bucket. If the distribution of balls by the lottery machine is truly random, then we would expect a similar number of balls in each bucket. Thus, if the lottery machine was set up to distribute 200 balls we would expect roughly 50 balls in each of the four buckets.

So, using the hypothetical data in Table 4.4 we can see that there is no difference across male/female patients and counsellor. The actual observed counts match the expected counts.[2]

Table 4.4 Group/counsellor cross-tabulation with no difference across males/females (hypothetical data)

Group * Counsellor Crosstabulation

			Counsellor John	Counsellor Jane	Total
Group	male	Count	50	50	100
		Expected Count	50.0	50.0	100.0
	female	Count	50	50	100
		Expected Count	50.0	50.0	100.0
Total		Count	100	100	200
		Expected Count	100.0	100.0	200.0

In Table 4.5 we have the opposite scenario: all the males saw John, whereas all the females saw Jane. Notice that the *expected* frequencies remain the same – 50 in each cell. The divergence from expected frequencies would strongly suggest that there is a relationship between sex of the patient and the counsellor they saw: we have *50 more male patients than expected* seeing John (and 50 less than expected seeing Jane); and *50 more female patients than expected* seeing Jane (and 50 less than expected seeing John).

Table 4.5 Group/counsellor cross-tabulation with a large difference across males/females (hypothetical data)

Group * Counsellor Crosstabulation

			Counsellor John	Counsellor Jane	Total
Group	male	Count	100	0	100
		Expected Count	50.0	50.0	100.0
	female	Count	0	100	100
		Expected Count	50.0	50.0	100.0
Total		Count	100	100	200
		Expected Count	100.0	100.0	200.0

What the chi-square statistic does is to calculate the odds of this distribution happening by chance.

Let us run chi-square on our counselling data and see what happens.

Running chi-square in SPSS

1 From the menu at the top of the screen click: **Analyze** then **Descriptive Statistics** then **Crosstabs**.
2 Move the variable **sex** into the rows box and **counsellor** into the columns box.
3 Click the **Cells** button. Ensure that *observed* and *expected* counts are ticked, and *row percentages* (since we want to know the percentages of males and females who saw each counsellor).

Screenshot 4.2

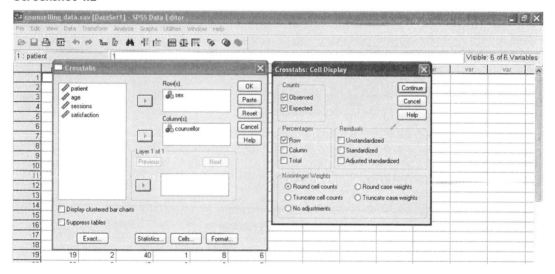

4 Click **Continue** to close this box.
5 Click on the **Statistics** tab and put a tick in the **chi-square** box.

Screenshot 4.3

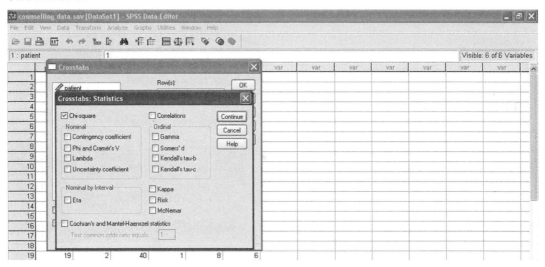

6   Click **Continue** then click **OK** to run the analysis.

The SPSS output viewer should produce the cross-tabulation table and a table listing the chi-square and related tests.

Note: SPSS can produce some scary output tables listing all kinds of statistics with obscure and complicated names which may or may not be relevant to your analysis. The chi-square test table is a mild example. The trick is to know what you are looking for, as will be illustrated.

Table 4.6 Cross-tabulation of sex and counsellor with expected counts

sex * counsellor Crosstabulation

			counsellor		Total
			John	Jane	
sex	male	Count	10	4	14
		Expected Count	6.5	7.5	14.0
		% within sex	71.4%	28.6%	100.0%
	female	Count	4	12	16
		Expected Count	7.5	8.5	16.0
		% within sex	25.0%	75.0%	100.0%
Total		Count	14	16	30
		Expected Count	14.0	16.0	30.0
		% within sex	46.7%	53.3%	100.0%

Table 4.7 Chi-square tests table

Chi-Square Tests

	Value	df	Asymp. Sig. (2-sided)	Exact Sig. (2-sided)	Exact Sig. (1-sided)
Pearson Chi-Square	6.467[b]	1	.011		
Continuity Correction [a]	4.736	1	.030		
Likelihood Ratio	6.709	1	.010		
Fisher's Exact Test				.026	.014
Linear-by-Linear Association	6.251	1	.012		
N of Valid Cases	30				

a. Computed only for a 2x2 table

b. 0 cells (.0%) have expected count less than 5. The minimum expected count is 6.53.

The first thing to note is the footnote (b) which tells us that '0 cells have expected count less that 5'. This is an important assumption of chi-square. If you are intending to cross-tabulate data and use the chi-square statistic, you should always try to ensure that you have a large enough sample size to maintain sufficient values in the cells.[3]

The values we are interested in are along the top *Pearson chi-square* row. The Pearson chi-square value is 6.467, with a significance or *probability* (p) value of .011. This means that, according to the chi-square calculation, the probability of this distribution of values occurring by chance is less than .01 – or 1 in 100, so probability (p) = .01. We would accept these odds as statistically significant and conclude that there is a relationship between the sex of patients and the counsellor they saw: male patients were more likely to see the male counsellor and female patients were more likely to see the female counsellor.[4]

So, in your report to the doctor you would first point out that cross-tabulation between the sex of patients and counsellors showed that a greater proportion tended to see the same sex counsellor: 71 per cent of male patients saw John; 75 per cent of female patients saw Jane. But then you would also add that the chi-square statistic showed this to be statistically significant: $\chi^2 = 6.467$, p = .011. You would then go on to comment on this result, for example possible explanations.

4.4 Levels of statistical significance

In discussing the outcomes of the chi-square analysis we have introduced an important concept – that of statistical significance. There is a convention in research that we may accept a 5 per cent (written as 0.05 which is 5 in 100, or 1 in 20) probability of accepting that there is a significant difference if it were true that there was really no difference (a false positive).

In actual fact, the chi-square test has calculated that the odds are 1 in 100 (.01) that this distribution of scores in the four cells could occur by chance. Looking at it another way, if you had a random lottery machine distributing balls into the four cells this result might occur one time in 100 trials using 30 balls.

We should, of course, adjust our acceptable level of statistical significance according to the context. For example, we might not want to accept a 1 in 20 (0.05) chance that an experimental drug with harmful side effects really has no power to reduce pain: 'Well, according to our trials, there's a 1/20 probability that it doesn't actually reduce pain, and the positive results we found were purely down to chance.' In this case we might well want to increase our level of significance to 1 in 100 (0.01) – at least!

The problem being that we have to strike a balance. The lower you set your criteria for significance, the more likely you are to conclude with a false positive – concluding that there *is* a significant difference when there is not in reality – in our counselling example, arguing for a male and female counsellor to cater for patient preferences when further research with a larger sample would show that there really is not a preference for same-sex counsellor. But conversely, if you set your threshold for significance too high, you are more likely to conclude with a false negative – saying there is no difference when there actually is. In statistics books these are known as Type I (false-positive) and Type II (false-negative) errors.

This also raises the issue of 'power' and 'effect size'. Imagine two experiments. The first aims to test the effects of a drug on humans which is known to be highly noxious through laboratory and animal experiments. What size sample would you need? Well, if we expect that the effect is going to be particularly distinctive – vomiting, convulsions, etc., then we would hope not very many. Hopefully, after say five people taking the drug and another five taking a placebo, we would have some pretty strong data comparing the two conditions.

But imagine a second experiment which is using a questionnaire to measure levels of anxiety before and after counselling. The researchers think that counselling will reduce the levels of anxiety for most patients, but possibly not by that much, and for some patients levels of anxiety may rise as they confront their issues. So the effect that we were expecting is not particularly distinctive in this case – and therefore we would need a much larger sample to avoid concluding with a false negative. This is the basis of 'power calculations' where, basically, the smaller the effect size, the larger the sample size needed.

Unfortunately then, there is no simple answer to the question, 'How large a sample do I need?' since it depends on the particular research you are conducting, the outcome measures you are using and the size of the effect you might be expecting.[5] As a general rule of thumb, you should be aiming for as large a sample as possible (to detect differences if they do exist), but not continuing the recruitment beyond that which is required to determine any effects you are investigating. Otherwise you will be wasting your time and your patients' time which, furthermore, may be regarded as unethical particularly where there may be adverse effects – as in the example of testing a noxious drug.

In practice, there are often limitations in terms of time, resources and the available sample. For example, if there are only 30 referrals to a counselling service during the year, and you need to evaluate the service after a year, then that is your sample. Alternatively, if this is deemed to be too small a sample for your purposes (to provide meaningful results) then you would have to extend the recruitment period until you achieved a larger sample. Now let us move on to something simpler and more enjoyable – re-coding the data.

4.5 Re-coding interval variables into categorical variables

In our data we have only two categorical variables that we could cross-tabulate: sex of patients and counsellors (and we've done that). Sometimes, however, it is useful to transform interval variables into categories so that they can be cross-tabulated with existing categorical variables. As we will see in the following exercise, and the exercises at the end of this chapter, grouping interval data into categories can reveal interesting comparisons that would not otherwise be apparent.

For example, we might wish to cross-tabulate sex and age of patients. Obviously we are unable to do this because the age data is not in categories – we would end up with as many categories as there are ages! What we could do, however, is to put the ages into categories, say 20–9, 30–9, 40–9, and then cross-tabulate the *age categories* with sex of patients. In SPSS we do this by re-coding variables.

Re-coding age into categories

1 From the menu at the top of the screen click **Transform** then **Recode into different variables**. This should produce the dialogue box shown. (Note: If we had chosen 'Into same variables' our re-coding would *over-write* the existing data; not a good choice!)
2 Next put the variable **age** into the **Input Variable** box (the title of this box changes to **Numeric Variable** after you put **age** into it).
3 Under **Output Variable** on the right side of the box type in a name for the new age variable you will be creating. I have used **agecats** to stand for age categories, and added a fuller description below in the **Label** box: age categories.
4 Click **Change** and this will then appear in the **Numeric Variable/Output Variable** box.

Screenshot 4.4

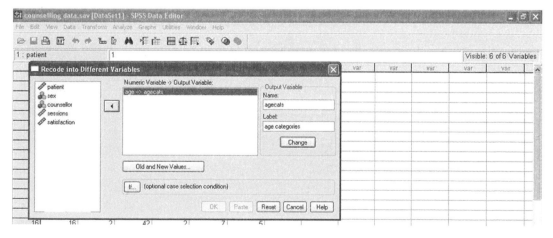

5 Click **Old and New Values** to open the recode dialogue box.
6 Click in the circle next to **Range** to enter age categories. In our data, age ranges from 21 to 49, so we will use the following categories: 20–9, 30–9, 40–9.
7 First enter 20, then 29 (as shown below), then in the **New Value** box type in 1. You have assigned the number 1 to the age category 20–9.

Screenshot 4.5

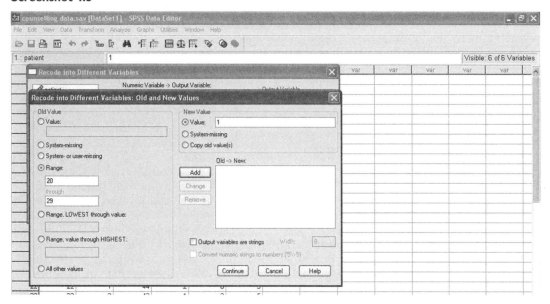

8 Now click **Add** and this will be entered into the **Old–New** variable box below.
9 Continue until you have assigned numbers to all the age categories, as illustrated next:

Screenshot 4.6

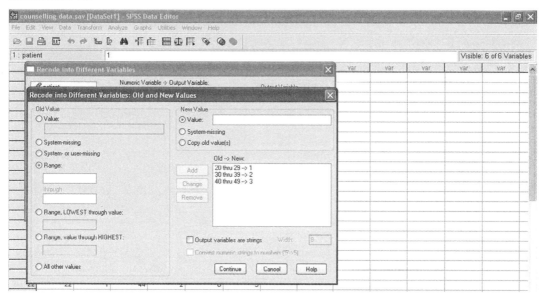

10 Click **Continue**, then click **OK** on the next screen. Your database will now have an additional variable that you have created called **agecats**. (If your new variable includes decimal places, remove them in **Variable View**.)

Screenshot 4.7

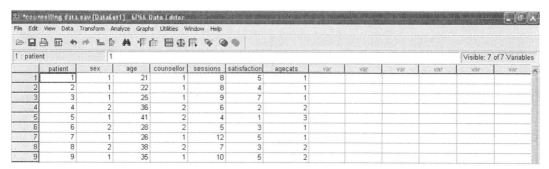

11 Be sure to check that you have conducted this procedure correctly – that your categories actually match, i.e., check that a 1 in agecats is within the range 20–9 in the age variable, that a 2 – 30–9 and a 3 = 40–9.
12 You should then add value labels to your age categories – by going into the **Variable View** and clicking on **Values** (as described in Chapter 2). You should also change the **Measure** from **Scale** to **Ordinal**.
13 Once you have added value labels, you can run crosstabs on **sex** and **agecat** by going to **Analyze** then **Descriptive Statistics** then **Crosstabs**. Move **sex** into Rows and **agecats** into Columns. Then click on the **Cells** tab and check that there is a tick in the box next to **Observed counts** and **row percentages** in the **Crosstabs: Cell Display** box as illustrated next:

Screenshot 4.8

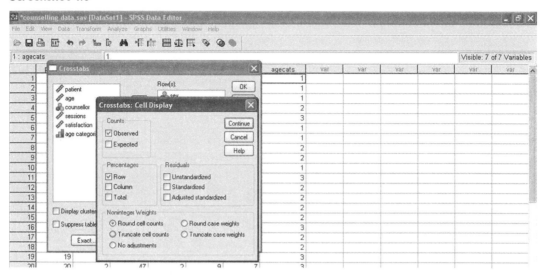

14 Click **Continue**, then **OK**.

This should produce the following table:

Table 4.8 Cross-tabulation of sex with age categories

sex * agecats Crosstabulation

			agecats			
			20-29	30-39	40-49	Total
sex	male	Count	5	7	2	14
		% within sex	35.7%	50.0%	14.3%	100.0%
	female	Count	2	7	7	16
		% within sex	12.5%	43.8%	43.8%	100.0%
Total		Count	7	14	9	30
		% within sex	23.3%	46.7%	30.0%	100.0%

Although the numbers in each category are small, we might note that the males tended to be younger than the females. While there were similar percentages in the 30–9 age range, there were differences in the younger and older age categories: 36 per cent of males were in their 20s compared to only 12.5 per cent of females; 44 per cent of females were in their 40s compared to only 14 per cent of males.

Transforming data like age into categories can sometimes provide interesting information that would not be otherwise apparent. For example, a simple comparison of the mean age of male and female patients reveals that the mean age of males was 31 years and the mean age of females was 39 years. But all this tells us is that, on average, females were older. By transforming age into categories and cross-tabulating with sex we can actually see where these differences lie in terms of specific age groups.

There is just one more thing to note: because we have created three categories of age the numbers are even fewer in the six cells. Many students go on to report the chi-square statistic for this analysis. However, the numbers really are too small to produce a reliable chi-square, as you would see from the chi-square tests table, which cautions that '4 cells (67%) have expected count less than 5'. In such cases we can only report the cross-tabulation percentages showing this trend, and perhaps recommend a larger sample for statistical analysis.

4.6 Summary

In this chapter you have learnt about:

- How to cross-tabulate categorical data in SPSS.
- How to produce the chi-square statistical test.
- The concept of statistical significance, levels of significance, Type I (false positive) and Type II errors (false-negative) errors, and issues relating to power and 'effect size'.
- How to re-code interval variables into categorical variables.

4.7 Exercises

Exercise 4.1 Re-code counselling sessions into categories

Re-code the data for number of counselling sessions into three equal groups representing 'low', 'medium' and 'high' attendance and first cross-tabulate with 'counsellor' then with 'sex'. What do these cross-tabulations show?

Exercise 4.2 Re-code satisfaction ratings into categories

Re-code the data for satisfaction ratings into categories representing 'positive', 'negative' and 'neutral' ratings. Cross-tabulate this new variable with 'counsellor' then 'sex'. What is the best way to categorize satisfaction ratings into these categories? What do these cross-tabulations show?

Exercise 4.3 Can you do a chi-square with just this data?

Imagine that the doctor had managed to do some of his own analysis and came to you for some specific advice. He has actually counted up the number of patients who came to see John and Jane and noticed that the majority of males saw John and the majority of females saw Jane. He shows you this in the following table:

Table 4.9 Number of patients who have seen each counsellor

	John	Jane	Total
Male	10	4	14
Female	4	12	16
Total	14	16	30

And while the doctor is quite pleased with this table, he wants to know if there is a statistic you can do on this data.

'Sure there is,' you say, 'it's called chi-square'.

'That's great you're so knowledgeable,' replies the doctor, 'can you put these figures into your computer and tell me what the chi-square statistic says?'

Well, can you?

Now you might be thinking, as I did for years, that you would need to enter all the raw data for the 30 patients into SPSS to do a chi-square. Well you would be wrong! Here is how you do it:

1   Open a new file and in **Variable View** create variables for 'sex' and 'counsellor'; these should be 'string variables'. Then create a third variable (numeric) for the observed frequencies.

You should then enter the data from the above table using a row for each combination of the two categories; then for each combination you enter the frequencies as illustrated below:

Screenshot 4.9

2   Now, and here is the clever bit, we need to tell SPSS that the numbers in the frequencies column represent the total number of observations for that combination of categories (they are not just values for another variable). To do this you have to go to **Data / Weight Cases**, then select **Weight cases by**, and move **frequencies** into the **Frequency Variable** box:

Screenshot 4.10

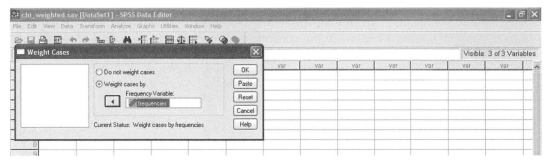

3 When you have done this, click **OK** and you can run your chi-square test as described earlier in this chapter. It is so much easier than entering all the raw data.

4.8 Notes

1 This information might also be relevant for any further analysis. For example, if we found that one counsellor received higher satisfaction ratings than the other, it could be that females are more generous in their ratings than males. It could even be that same-sex patients and counsellors worked best – achieving the highest satisfaction ratings. It is factors like these that need to be investigated in quantitative data analysis.

2 Expected frequencies for each cell are calculated by multiplying row total by column total and dividing by the grand total. So, the expected frequency for the top right cell in Table 4.4 (50) is arrived at through the following calculation: $(100 \times 100)/200 = 50$. The same values apply to all the cells in this table of course.

3 What is a large enough sample size? Well, for this chi-square our sample of 30 was just enough given the distribution of the male and female patients. One source recommends a sample of at least 50 (Watson *et al.* 2006), but the point is that you need to maintain sufficient numbers in each of the cells, so the sample needs to be fairly evenly distributed across the categories.

4 Some authors recommend citing the more conservative continuity correction (second line down in the table) for 2×2 tables like this one (i.e. two row categories – male/female, and two column categories – John/Jane), but Pett (1997: 163) and Howell (1997: 149) advise against citing this value. Some authors also suggest that where expected frequencies are less than 5 in 2×2 tables, we can cite the more conservative Fisher's Exact Test (fourth line down in the table) instead of the Pearson chi-square value (Pett 1997; Kinnear and Gray 2004). However, Howell (1997: 152) points out that the chi-square is robust to violations from small sample sizes and is unlikely to produce false positive results (i.e., concluding a significant difference when there is not one). Indeed, the problem with small sample sizes is that they are more likely to have insufficient numbers (or 'power') to show a significant difference.

5   There are techniques (and some computer programs) to determine sample sizes that rely on estimates of effect from previous similar research using similar outcome measures. The idea being that if we know the size of the effect to expect from previous studies then we can calculate the size of the sample needed to ensure a sufficient sample size to detect significant differences if they exist. This is beyond the scope of this book but for a relatively simple estimate of sample sizes needed, Cohen (1988) includes some tables which enable you to estimate sample size depending on the size of the effect you want to detect. 'The size of the effect you want to detect' requires a decision on your part as to what constitutes a meaningful difference. For example, if you are evaluating the effect of a counselling service on patients mental health, then you need to decide what would constitute a meaningful improvement in mental health on your outcome measure. If the scale goes from 1–100, where 100 represents optimum mental well-being, what do you consider is a minimally important clinical difference on the scale to signal real improvement in mental health? If you agree that it is a rise of ten points on the scale then that is the size of the effect you are looking to detect.

5 Correlation: examining relationships between interval data

In this chapter you will learn about scatterplots and correlation to examine the direction and strength of relationships between variables.

5.1 Introduction

In Chapter 1 we briefly discussed the possibility of conducting correlation analysis on our data. We saw that correlation describes the direction and strength of a relationship between two interval variables (e.g., height and shoe size) and that the direction can be positive or negative:

- Positive correlation: an increase in values for one variable is associated with an increase in values for the other variable, for example, as height increases so does shoe size.
- Negative correlation: an increase in values for one variable is associated with a decrease in values on another variable, for example, as temperature *reduces* the use of electricity for heating *increases*.

In order to demonstrate this, scatterplots were used to graphically illustrate the relationship between values for two variables. For example, Figure 1.4 (repeated in Figure 5.1 on the next page) showed quite a strong positive correlation between height and shoe size – the strength being determined by how tightly the plot forms a line rising from left to right.

5.2 Examining correlations in the questionnaire

Turning to our questionnaire, we first need to identify two interval variables that might be correlated. We have three to choose from:

- age of patients;
- number of sessions;
- satisfaction ratings.

Looking at these three variables, the obvious choice for correlation is number of sessions and satisfaction ratings since we might assume that the more appointments a patient had, the more satisfied they would be with the counselling. But, as was suggested in Chapter 1, perhaps it does not work like this – maybe more appointments are linked to more unresolved problems and thus less satisfaction? Well, let us have a look at the data and see.

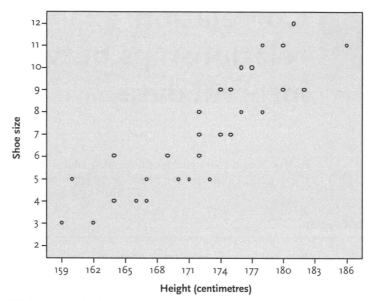

Figure 5.1 Scatterplot for height and shoe size

5.2.1 Producing a scatterplot in SPSS

The first thing we should do is produce a scatterplot of the data.

1 From the menu click on **Graphs**, then **Chart Builder**.
2 Select **Scatter/Dot** from the **Gallery** to show the range of graphs available and then drag the first 'simple scatter' graph into the preview area.
3 Drag **satisfaction** into the Y-axis box and **sessions** into the X-axis box – as illustrated on the next page:

Screenshot 5.1

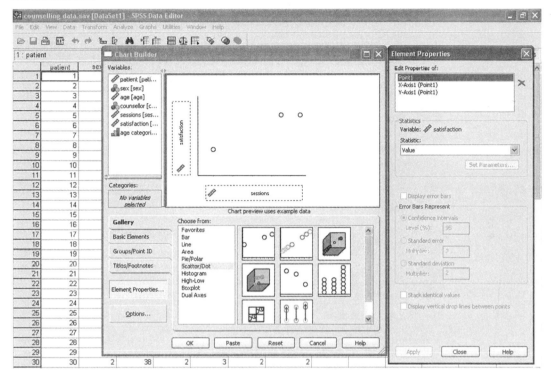

4   Click **OK**.

This should produce the output displayed in the scatterplot below (see Figure 5.2):

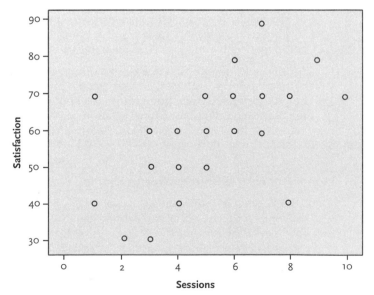

Figure 5.2 Scatterplot of sessions and satisfaction ratings

Note: In SPSS v15 you may need to use Chart Editor to change the Y-Axis scale in order to provide a 5% lower margin for the lower values: double-click on the Y-Axis and in the Properties box change Lower margin (%) from 0 to 5.

From the scatterplot we can immediately discern a pattern rising from left to right suggesting that the two variables are positively correlated: patients who attended for more counselling sessions reported higher levels of satisfaction.

5.2.2 The strength of a correlation

Now while it is important to produce scatterplots like this to see if two variables *look* like they are correlated, this is only half the story. The next step is to apply a statistical test to this data to determine the strength of this correlation and whether or not it is statistically significant (unlikely to have occurred by chance).

The strength of a correlation is indicated on a scale ranging from −1 to +1 as illustrated in Table 5.1:

Table 5.1 The strength of a correlation

Negative correlation			Positive correlation		
−1 −.9 −.8 −.7 −.6 −.5 −.4 −.3 −.2 −.1		**0**	.1 .2 .3 .4 .5 .6 .7 .8 .9 +1		
Strong negative	Weak positive		Weak positive	Strong positive	

As a general guideline, a value ranging from 0.1 to 0.4 would be classed as a weak correlation, and anything above 0.5 would be regarded as a strong correlation (Cohen, 1988). A value approaching zero indicates the absence of any relationship between two variables, in other words no correlation.

You would only find a perfect positive correlation (+1) where there is a one-to-one incremental relationship between the two variables, for example, number of cinema tickets sold and customers in audience (assuming no one has sneaked in without buying a ticket of course). Obviously this level of correlation (perfect correlation) is unlikely in health and social research.

So, the next question is how do we obtain this value for the strength of a correlation from SPSS? Well, for our two variables with interval data – counselling sessions and satisfaction ratings, the appropriate measure of correlation is the Pearson product-moment correlation coefficient.[1] Though see Box 5.1 for a key assumption in using the Pearson correlation test.

Box 5.1 Non-linear relationship between variable

A scatterplot is important not only to see if there looks to be a relationship between two variables but also what *type* of relationship. The Pearson product-moment correlation coefficient is a measure of linear (straight line) relationships between two variables so would not be appropriate for measuring the strength of a relationship that takes a different form. Figure 5.3 below provides an example of a non-linear – curvilinear – relationship.

When I ask students in class what this graph might represent, a number of interesting options are suggested. One mature student suggested, somewhat morosely, that it could represent number of years married and level of happiness . . .

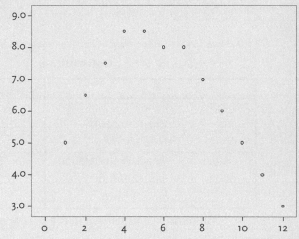

Figure 5.3 Scatterplot showing a curvilinear relationship

Running the Pearson correlation

1 From the menu at the top of the screen click: **Analyze / Correlate / Bivariate** (*bi* meaning two and *variate* meaning variable).
2 Move **sessions** and **satisfaction** into the variables box.
3 Ensure that the **Pearson** box is ticked.

Screenshot 5.2

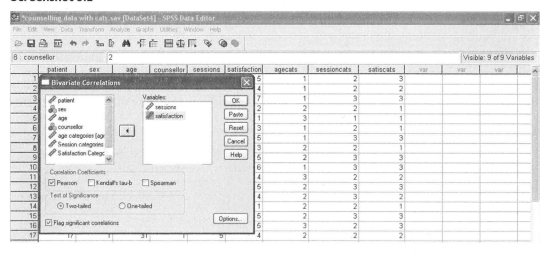

4 Click **OK**.

This should produce the following output table showing that the Pearson correlation between sessions and satisfaction is 0.53. So we have quite a strong positive correlation. The information below this in the row labelled **Sig. (2-tailed)** tells us that the correlation is statistically significant at the 0.003 level. It is therefore unlikely to have occurred by chance (the concept of statistical significance was discussed in Chapter 4).[2]

Table 5.2 Pearson correlations between sessions and satisfaction

Correlations

		sessions	satisfaction
sessions	Pearson Correlation	1	.530**
	Sig. (2-tailed)	.	.003
	N	30	30
satisfaction	Pearson Correlation	.530**	1
	Sig. (2-tailed)	.003	.
	N	30	30

**. Correlation is significant at the 0.01 level (2-tailed).

When you write-up the results of this analysis in a report you should refer to the value for the strength of the Pearson correlation coefficient as 'r', as illustrated below:

We can therefore conclude that there is a strong positive correlation between the two variables (r = .53, p = .003), with a greater number of sessions being associated with a higher satisfaction rating.

5.2.3 The coefficient of determination

But what does this 'strong correlation' of 0.53 actually mean in terms of 'predicting' one value from another? In other words, to what extent can we say that patient satisfaction ratings are related to the number of counselling sessions?

There is a simple calculation we can perform to answer this question. It is referred to as the coefficient of determination (r^2), and provides a measure of the degree to which one variable 'predicts' the other by simply squaring the correlation value. You can then simply multiply this by 100 to give a percentage value.

For example, if you conducted a correlation between monthly salary and annual salary this should yield a perfect positive correlation, in other words, r = 1.0. If you square this figure (1 × 1 = 1) and multiply by 100 this shows 100 per cent predictability: if you know monthly salary you can accurately predict annual salary.

So, turning back to our counselling data, first, we square our value of 0.53 to get the value of 0.28, and then we multiply this by 100 to arrive at the percentage value of 28 per cent. So in fact, our 'strong correlation' of 0.5 actually means that only 28 per cent of the variance in satisfaction ratings is related to counselling sessions. We should therefore conclude that satisfaction ratings *are* related to the number of counselling sessions but this only accounts for 28 per cent of the variance; there are other factors involved. See Box 5.2 for a real world example of correlation and the use of this coefficient of determination value.

Box 5.2 Correlation and the coefficient of determination: a real world example

I was recently involved in a research project evaluating the provision of welfare advice in 30 general practices (family practices or health centres for those outside the UK). Welfare advice workers attended at the general practices for one morning or afternoon each week to help patients referred to them (by the doctor or nurses) for assistance with things like claiming welfare benefits (e.g., disability allowances).

After two years we found that the number of referrals to the advice workers varied quite significantly across the 30 practices, ranging from 16 to 234 (mean: 80; median: 69). This meant that at some practices demand for welfare advice was outstripping supply while at others the advice worker was not being used to their full capacity.

Anecdotally, it was suggested that this disparity in the number of referrals across the practices was due to varying levels of engagement with the service: some practices were pleased to host the extra service for their patients, and therefore made referrals, but others were not, so failed to refer.

However, another reason was suggested by one of the practice managers: perhaps this variation in the number of referrals simply reflects the patient list size of the practices? We then found out that patient list size of the 30 practices ranged from 1768 to 7102 and that there was indeed a positive correlation between list size and number of referrals: $r = .75$, $p = .005$. However, using the coefficient of determination calculation we can see that patient list size only accounted for 56 per cent of the variance in referrals across the practices, so other factors like engagement with the service still needed to be explored.

The coefficient of determination value also draws our attention to an important issue in interpreting and comparing correlation values: a correlation of 0.8 is not twice as strong as a correlation of 0.4. Thus if we calculate the coefficient of determination values we find that a correlation of 0.4 indicates that 16 per cent of the variance in one variable is accounted for by the other variable, but a correlation of 0.8 indicates that 64 per cent of the variance in one variable is accounted for by the other.

5.3 Summary

In this chapter you have learnt how to:

• Examine relationships between two interval variables to see if they are positively or negatively correlated.

- Produce scatterplots to graphically illustrate the relationship between two variables.
- Conduct the Pearson product-moment correlation to examine the statistical strength and direction of a linear correlation.
- Interpret the strength of a correlation using the coefficient of determination.

In the following exercises you will also learn about:

- The importance of sample sizes in correlation and obtaining statistically significant results.
- How outliers can have a significant influence on correlation statistics.
- The importance of distinguishing between correlation and cause.

5.4 Exercises

Exercise 5.1 Produce scatterplots and correlations for the other interval variables

Conduct correlations for (a) age and number of sessions; and (b) age and satisfaction with the service. Remember to produce a scatterplot for the data before running the Pearson correlation. What do the results show in terms of (a) the strength and direction of any correlations; and (b) the statistical significance of the results?

Exercise 5.2 The importance of sample sizes in correlation

Sample sizes can have a profound effect on statistical significance. Try running the Pearson correlation between *age* and *number of sessions* again, but this time with double the number of cases for each of these variables.

Highlight the 30 cases for **age**, right-click the mouse button and copy, then move your cursor to the end of the data column for **age** (row 31) and paste in the data you have copied. So you have the same data but double the number of cases. Next, follow the same procedure for **sessions**. Then run the Pearson correlation on the 60 cases for age and sessions.

Exercise 5.3 The importance of 'outliers' in correlation

There is another reason why you should always produce a scatterplot of the data if you are looking for correlations: to identify outliers – any data points that are out on their own away from the main cluster. These can have a significant influence on any correlation statistics.

Have a look at the scatterplot for *age* and *satisfaction* again (you should have produced it for Exercise 5.1b). Are there any outliers? Imagine trying to draw an oval, fat cigar shape around the dots in the scatterplot to discern a negative correlation – is there one dot in particular that falls outside your oval shape? If so, identify the case number, remove it from your dataset (values for age and satisfaction), and run the Pearson correlation again.

Exercise 5.4 Explain the following correlations[3]

(a) It is reported that there is a strong positive correlation between ice cream sales and crime rates. Do we therefore conclude that ice cream causes crime?

(b) It is reported that there is a positive correlation between number of counselling sessions and level of psychological well-being? Can we therefore conclude that counselling works and more counselling works better?

(c) Consumption of milk is positively correlated to cancer. So does drinking milk cause cancer?

(d) Studies have found a negative correlation between smoking and Alzheimer's dementia: the risk of getting Alzheimer's dementia reduces with increased smoking of cigarettes. Would you therefore recommend that people start smoking or increase the number they smoke to prevent the onset of Alzheimer's dementia?

5.5 Notes

1 The other options are to use Kendall's tau or Spearman's test for correlations with ordinal level data.

2 And if you are wondering why it says '2-tailed', this will be explained in the next chapter.

3 Exercise 5.4(b) is taken from Watson *et al.* (2006). Exercises (c) and (d) are taken from Coolidge (2006).

6 Examining differences between two sets of scores

In this chapter you will learn about tests which tell us if there is a statistically significant difference between two sets of scores. In so doing you will learn about independent and dependent variables, parametric and non-parametric data, and independent and related samples.

6.1 Introduction

In this chapter we will look at statistical tests which tell us if there is a significant difference between two sets of scores. For example, this could be scores on an aptitude test comparing a sample of *males* and *females*, or scores *before* and *after* some intervention, e.g., mental health scores before and after a course of therapy for a sample of patients.

So, what differences between two sets of scores might we examine in our counselling questionnaire? In order to think about this it is useful to categorize variables into two kinds: *independent variables* and *dependent variables* (as discussed in Chapter 1). For example, we might think that satisfaction with the service is *dependent* on which counsellor the patient saw, in which case we would have the following *independent* and *dependent variables*:

- *Independent variable*: counsellor (John or Jane).
- *Dependent variable*: satisfaction rating.

In the counselling questionnaire there are in fact only two possible independent variables – the categorical variables *counsellor* and *sex*, and each has three possible dependent variables, as listed below:

1 *Independent variable*: counsellor (John or Jane):

- *dependent variable*: satisfaction ratings;
- *dependent variable*: number of sessions;
- *dependent variable*: age of patients.

2 *Independent variable*: sex (male or female):

- *dependent variable*: satisfaction ratings;
- *dependent variable*: number of sessions;
- *dependent variable*: age of patients.

Box 6:1 provides further discussion of independent and dependent variables in the context of experimental studies.

Having identified our independent and dependent variables, the next question is which differences do we wish to examine? And the answer to that is, which do we think are the most relevant? In my opinion we should start by comparing satisfaction ratings for the two counsellors, and then the number of sessions provided by each of the counsellors, since these might provide the most relevant information for the doctor who has commissioned this analysis.

Box 6.1 Experiments, variables and hypothesis testing

The concept of independent and dependent variables is really more relevant to experiments where the investigator manipulates the independent variable to see the effect on the dependent variable. Indeed the independent variable is sometimes referred to as the *treatment variable*. For example, the investigator might manipulate the type of treatment offered to patients (randomly assigning patients to a particular treatment) and measure the outcomes. Type of treatment would be the independent variable (e.g., physiotherapy compared to acupuncture) and the outcome (e.g., level of back pain) would be the dependent variable. Alternatively, the investigator might manipulate the *level* of treatment, for example the dosage of a drug, and compare the outcomes dependent on the dosage administered.

In such circumstances we may formulate an experimental hypothesis which makes a prediction about the relationship between the independent and dependent variables, for example:

> *Hypothesis*: acupuncture will lead to greater reductions in the level of back pain than physiotherapy.

And having proposed an experimental hypothesis we should also formulate what is referred to as a 'null hypothesis' stating the absence of a relationship between the independent variable and the dependent variable, for example:

> *Null Hypothesis*: there will be no difference between acupuncture and physiotherapy on the level of back pain experienced by patients.

The results of our experiment will enable us to either retain or reject the null hypothesis. So, if we find that acupuncture did indeed lead to greater reductions in the level of pain we conclude that the null hypothesis was rejected. If there was no difference, then we conclude that the null hypothesis was not rejected.

Confounding variables

Another factor we need to take into account is the potential role of extraneous or confounding variables. These are variables other than the independent variable that may have affected the outcomes on the dependent variable. For example, if we found that acupuncture was better than physiotherapy in reducing back pain there might be other factors that have contributed to this outcome: perhaps the acupuncturist had more sessions with patients; perhaps the patients who saw the acupuncturist were younger with less chronic problems that were more amenable to treatment, etc. Issues such as these highlight the importance of controlling the conditions in the design of experiments, in this hypothetical example, at least ensuring the same amount of sessions and a comparable sample of patients.

6.2 Comparing satisfaction ratings for the two counsellors

In order to compare the satisfaction ratings for the two counsellors we first need to choose the appropriate statistical test. Statistical tests comparing scores between two samples (in our study, satisfaction ratings for John vs satisfaction ratings for Jane) fall into two categories depending on the type of data we have. Figure 6.1 illustrates the decision process for choosing the appropriate statistical test.

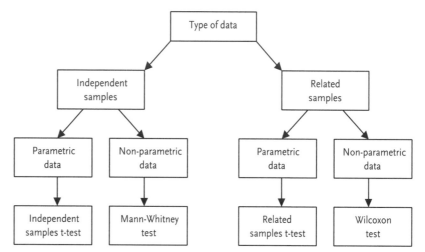

Figure 6.1 Choosing the appropriate statistical test for differences between two samples

6.2.1 Independent or related samples?

The first thing we need to know is whether our data comes from two independent samples or two related samples. Related samples are those where the *same people provide two sets of scores*. For example, in our data the doctor might have asked patients to complete a mental health questionnaire measuring their levels of anxiety *before* and *after* counselling; the idea being to see if the counselling has any effect on the scores – hopefully reducing levels of anxiety/depression.[1]

It should be apparent then, that our data comparing patient satisfaction ratings for the two counsellors is not related. Rather, the satisfaction ratings for each counsellor will come from two independent groups of people: those patients who saw John and those who saw Jane.

6.2.2 Parametric or non-parametric test?

Having followed the arrow in Figure 6.1 to *independent samples* we now need to decide whether to use a test for parametric or non-parametric data.

Parametric tests assume certain characteristics (parameters) of the population from which the sample is drawn. In general, parametric tests should only be used when the following conditions apply:

1 Level of measurement is interval or ratio (more than ordinal).
2 The scores approximate a normal distribution.
3 The variance (spread of scores) within both groups is relatively similar (homogeneity of variance).

Non-parametric tests do not depend on these assumptions. Wherever possible you should choose the parametric test because it is *more powerful*. This means that it is more sensitive than the non-parametric test in discerning significant differences in two scores.[2]

So, we know that our data is from independent samples, and we also know that it is interval (satisfaction ratings), what we next need to find out is whether or not the data is normally distributed. The simplest way to do this is by producing histograms to see if the data looks like it approximates a normal distribution.

Producing histograms to check for normal distributions

1 From the menu at the top of the screen click on **Graphs** then **Chart Builder**.
2 Select **Histogram** from the **Gallery** and drag the first (Simple) **Histogram** into the preview area.
3 Drag the variable **satisfaction** to the X-axis.
4 Click **Groups/Point ID** and put a tick in the **Rows** panel ID checkbox.
5 This will produce a **Panel box** to the right of the preview area. Drag the variable **counsellor** into the **Panel box**.
6 Finally, to the right of your screen in the **Element Properties** section, place a tick in the box next to **Display normal curve** and then click **Apply**.
7 Click **OK**.

Screenshot 6.1

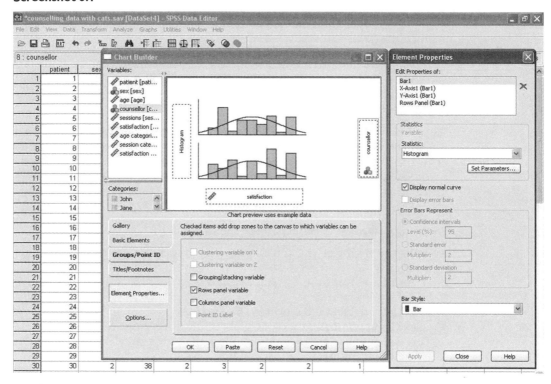

This should produce the two histograms below with lines showing that the data is relatively normally distributed, with most of the scores in the middle, tailing off at either end.

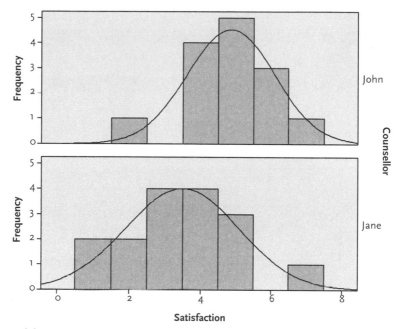

Figure 6.2 Histograms showing satisfaction ratings for each counsellor

Now, many researchers will be quite happy to visually examine the data from histograms to see that the data approximates a normal distribution and leave it at that. Remember, it just needs to *approximate* a normal distribution because the test is robust to 'moderate departures'. But, as Field (2005) points out, this can be quite subjective and open to abuse ('Well, it looked normal to me'). So, for a more objective measure of whether a distribution is normal we may refer to two further tests: Kolmogorov-Smirnov and Shapiro-Wilk. If the results of these tests are statistically significant then this suggests that the distribution deviates significantly from a normal distribution.

Producing a test of normality

1 From the menu at the top of the screen click on **Analyze** then **Descriptives** then **Explore**.
2 Move **satisfaction** into the Dependent list and **counsellor** into the Factor list.
3 Under **Display** ensure that there is only a tick next to **Plots**.
4 Click on the **Plots** tab to open the plots dialogue box.
5 Under **Boxplots** click **None**, and remove any ticks under **Descriptive**. Place a tick in **Normality** plots with tests. Under **Spread vs Level** tick **none**.
6 Click **Continue**, then **OK**.

Screenshot 6.2

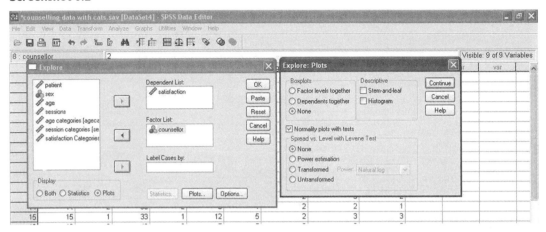

This will produce an output table of the tests of normality along with a number of graphs. We will focus on the statistics in the table: since neither of these tests includes any significant results (0.05 or less in the sig. columns) this confirms our observations from the histograms, in other words, that our data is sufficiently normally distributed.

Table 6.1 Tests of normality

Tests of Normality

		Kolmogorov-Smirnov[a]			Shapiro-Wilk		
	counsellor	Statistic	df	Sig.	Statistic	df	Sig.
satisfaction	John	.189	14	.189	.923	14	.241
	Jane	.127	16	.200*	.951	16	.508

*. This is a lower bound of the true significance.

a. Lilliefors Significance Correction

So, having (thoroughly) checked that the data is normally distributed, we are able to follow the arrow in Figure 6.1 to the (parametric) independent samples t-test.

Running an independent samples t-test

1 From the menu at the top of the screen click **Analyze** then **Compare Means** then **Independent samples t-test**.
2 Move **satisfaction** into **Test Variable**.
3 Move **counsellor** into **Grouping Variable**.
4 Click **Define Groups** (since your Grouping Variable is **counsellor**, you need to specify a numerical value for each, in other words, 1 for John, 2 for Jane).
5 Enter the value 1 (for John) in Group 1 and value 2 (for Jane) in Group 2.

Screenshot 6.3

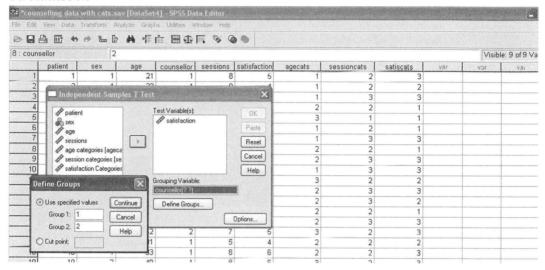

6   Click **Continue** then click **OK**.

You should then be presented with the following (rather scary) output.

Table 6.2 Group statistics

Group Statistics

	counsellor	N	Mean	Std. Deviation	Std. Error Mean
satisfaction	John	14	4.00	1.231	.329
	Jane	16	3.50	1.592	.398

Table 6.3 Independent samples test

Independent Samples Test

		Levene's Test for Equality of Variances		t-test for Equality of Means							
										95% Confidence Interval of the Difference	
		F	Sig.	t	df	Sig. (2-tailed)	Mean Difference	Std. Error Difference	Lower	Upper
satisfaction	Equal variances assumed	1.209	.281	2.583	28	.015	1.357	.525	.281	2.433
	Equal variances not assumed			2.628	27.626	.014	1.357	.516	.299	2.416

The group statistics table (Table 6.2) shows the number of students in each category and the mean values, from which we can see that the mean score for John was 4.86 compared to 3.50 for Jane.

The table also provides us with the standard deviation of the scores for each group. This is the average deviation from the mean for each group of scores – providing a measure of the spread of the scores. Notice that the standard deviation of satisfaction ratings for Jane is slightly larger than those for John. This is graphically displayed in the boxplots (below) where we can see that the spread of scores is slightly greater in the ratings for Jane.

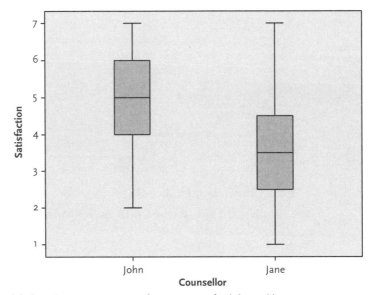

Figure 6.3 Boxplots comparing satisfaction ratings for John and Jane

So we can see that the satisfaction ratings were higher for patients who went to see John, but is this a statistically significant difference?

The independent samples test output table (Table 6.3), first provides Levene's test for equality of variances. Recall that 'homogeneity of variance' was one of the assumptions required for using a parametric test – so this is checking that the variance (spread of scores) within both groups of scores (ratings for John and Jane) is relatively similar. Since the value for this test is *not significant* (0.281 is larger than our significance level of 0.05), this means we have not violated this assumption and we can proceed by examining the first line of this table – equal variances assumed (violation would mean citing the slightly more conservative bottom line of the table). The column headed **Sig. (2-tailed)** tells us if the difference in the two means is statistically significant (the difference in the two means (1.357) being provided in the next column). Since this value is 0.015, and therefore a smaller value than our conventional significance level of 0.05, we may conclude that there was a significant difference in scores from the two groups. We might write this up in a report thus:

An independent samples t-test was used to examine differences in satisfaction ratings for each of the counsellors. The results showed that ratings for John were higher (M = 4.86; SD = 1.23) than those for Jane (M = 3.5; SD = 1.59); t = 2.58, p = .015.

Box 6.2 One-tailed and two-tailed tests

In statistics we can select 1-tailed and 2-tailed significance levels. A '2-tailed' significance level relates to a non-directional hypothesis. So, in this particular example our hypothesis (prediction) might have been: there will be a difference in satisfaction ratings for the two counsellors. It is '2-tailed' because we are not specifying whether the ratings for Jane will be higher or those for John – just that there will be a difference (either way). This is in contrast to a '1-tailed' significance level where the direction of the outcome has been specified, for example: satisfaction ratings for Jane will be higher than those for John. In general the 2-tailed significance level is cited since you can rarely be certain of the outcome, despite any predictions.

Confidence intervals

The final column provides the 95 per cent confidence interval of the difference. The confidence intervals in this table provide a range of values, from 0.28 to 2.43. Essentially, this means that on 95 per cent of occasions, were our sampling repeated, it would be expected that the differences would lie within these parameters.

So, although the mean difference for our data was 1.36, the confidence intervals suggest that, if we repeated this data collection 100 times, we would expect to find a difference in satisfaction ratings for John and Jane between 0.28 and 2.43 on 95 per cent of occasions. Hence, we are 95 per cent confident that the difference would lie between 0.28 and 2.43.

These parameters can be instructive. Notice that the lowest value is 0.28. This means that we can only be confident that the difference in the ratings for the two counsellors is at least 0.28, which is not much. We may conclude that our relatively small sample has suggested a quite small significant difference, but a larger sample of students would be needed to increase our confidence in the actual size of the difference in scores.

6.3 Comparing the number of sessions for each counsellor

The next difference we decided to examine is the number of counselling sessions conducted by each counsellor. Is one offering more sessions than the other? Perhaps this could help to explain why one received higher satisfaction ratings?

As with the previous analysis, we first need to decide on the appropriate statistical test. Referring back to Figure 6.1 we know that we are dealing with two independent samples of data, so our next task is to find out if we should use a parametric or a non-parametric test. Repeat the procedure for producing histograms to check for a normal distribution:

1 From the menu at the top of the screen click on **Graphs** then **Chart Builder**.
2 Select **Histogram** from the **Gallery** and drag the first **Histogram** into the preview area.

3 Drag **sessions** to the X-axis.
4 Click **Groups/Point ID** and put a tick in the **Rows** panel **Variable checkbox**.
5 Drag the variable **counsellor** into the **Panel** box.
6 In the **Element Properties** section to the right of your screen, place a tick in the box next to **Display normal curve**.
7 Click **Apply** and then click **OK**.

This should produce the following histograms (I have altered the scale (and increments) in Chart Editor to match the maximum number of sessions which was 12):

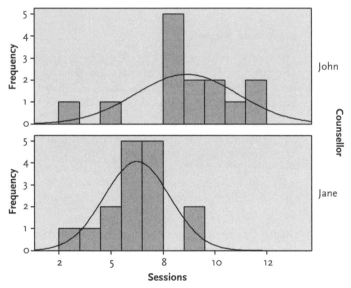

Figure 6.4 Histograms showing number of sessions for each counsellor

Now, although the 'normal curve' in these two histograms suggests that the data is normally distributed we can see that the actual data for John's sessions does appear to skew off towards the lower number of sessions. This illustrates how graphs, such as these, can be deceptive. Hence, if we modify the X-axis using Chart Editor to only include the actual range of sessions (1–12) we get a slightly different picture.

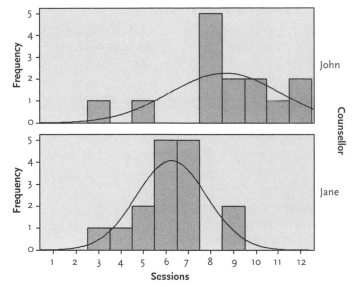

Figure 6.5 Scaled histograms showing number of sessions for each counsellor

From Figure 6.5 we can see that whereas the histogram for Jane approximates a normal distribution, the histogram for John's sessions suggests that the data is skewed towards the lower end. Thus we have a prime candidate for confirmation using the tests of normality statistics described above:

1 From the menu at the top of the screen click on **Analyze** then **Descriptives** then **Explore**.
2 Move **sessions** into the Dependent list and **counsellor** into the Factor list.
3 Under **Display** ensure that there is only a tick next to **Plots**.
4 Click on the **Plots** tab to open the plots dialogue box.
5 Under **Boxplots** click **None**, and remove any ticks under **Descriptive**. Place a tick in **Normality** plots with tests. **Under Spread vs Level** tick **none**.
6 Click **Continue**, then **OK**.

And, indeed, when we do produce the Tests of Normality we find that the Kolmogorov-Smirnov test is actually significant (0.014) suggesting that the distribution is significantly deviating from a normal distribution.

Table 6.4 Tests of normality

Tests of Normality

	counsellor	Kolmogorov-Smirnov[a]			Shapiro-Wilk		
		Statistic	df	Sig.	Statistic	df	Sig.
sessions	John	.254	14	.014	.910	14	.159
	Jane	.191	16	.120	.933	16	.275

a. Lilliefors Significance Correction *this is a lower bound of the true significance

This being the case, it might therefore be more appropriate to use the test for non-parametric data which, as illustrated in Figure 6.1, is the Mann-Whitney test.

Running the Mann-Whitney U test

1   From the menu at the top of the screen click **Analyze** then **Nonparametric Tests** then **2 Independent Samples**.

Screenshot 6.4

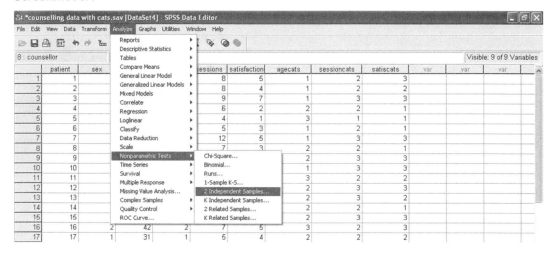

2   Move **sessions** into **Test Variable**.
3   Move **counsellor** into **Grouping Variable**.
4   Click **Define Groups** (since your Grouping Variable is counsellor, you need to specify the codes for the two groups, as we did for the t-test).
5   Enter the value 1 (for John) in Group 1 and value 2 (for Jane) in Group 2.
6   Click **Continue**.
7   Click the **Exact** tab to open the Exact tests dialogue box and click on the button next to **Exact** (the Exact test is more appropriate for smaller samples). Click **Continue**.

Screenshot 6.5

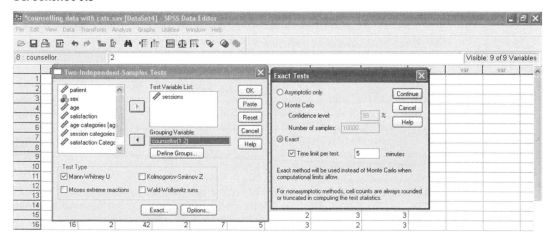

8   Ensure the Mann-Whitney U test is selected (it should be).
9   Click **OK**.

This should produce the following output:

Table 6.5 Mann-Whitney U test ranks

Ranks

	counsellor	N	Mean Rank	Sum of Ranks
sessions	John	14	20.61	288.50
	Jane	16	11.03	176.50
	Total	30		

Table 6.6 Mann-Whitney U test statistics

Test Statistics[b]

	sessions
Mann-Whitney U	40.500
Wilcoxon W	176.500
Z	-2.998
Asymp. Sig. (2-tailed)	.003
Exact Sig. [2*(1-tailed Sig.)]	.002[a]
Exact Sig. (2-tailed)	.002
Exact Sig. (1-tailed)	.001
Point Probability	.000

a. Not corrected for ties.

b. Grouping Variable: counsellor

The first table provides information about how the satisfaction ratings were ranked. The procedure for calculating the Mann-Whitney U statistic involves ranking all the scores from both groups in order of magnitude and then calculating the mean rank for each of the two groups. So, for John we can see that the mean ranking for his session is 20.61, but for Jane it is much lower at 11.03.

In the second table, the two values we are interested in are the Mann-Whitney U (40.5) and the Exact Significance level (Exact sig. (2-tailed)) which is $p = 0.002$. Since the probability (p value) of this result occurring by chance is lower than our conventional significance level of 0.05, we conclude that there is a significant difference in the number of sessions conducted by the two counsellors.

We would write-up the results of this analysis, first, by referring to the median number of counselling sessions conducted by the two counsellors – because the median, as we learned in Chapter 1, is more appropriate where the data is not normally distributed.[3] We would then proceed to cite the relevant statistics from the Mann-Whitney U Test. For example:

When the number of sessions conducted by the two counsellors was examined it was found that the median number of sessions conducted by John was 8.5 compared to 6.0 for Jane. The Mann-Whitney Test found this difference to be statistically significant: $U = 40.5$, $p = .002$.

This result might then be related to the higher satisfaction ratings for John, in other words, perhaps the higher satisfaction ratings related to the greater number of sessions he conducted with his patients?

Box 6.3 Comparing two sets of scores from related samples

In our counselling data we have used the relevant tests to compare two sets of scores from *independent samples*: the independent samples t-test for parametric data and the Mann-Whitney test for non-parametric data. But imagine if the doctor had also provided us with data from all the patients recording levels of anxiety before counselling and after counselling. For example, the doctor might have asked patients to rate their levels of anxiety (on an interval scale from 1–100) before the first session of counselling and then three months later. Since the data before and after counselling comes from the same people, we would have two sets of scores from *related samples*.

If the data satisfies the conditions for a parametric test then you should conduct the paired-samples t-test (as was indicated in Figure 6.1) by going to the menu at the top of the screen and clicking **Analyze / Compare Means / Paired-Samples T Test**. Then you need to highlight *both* variables and move them into the **Paired Variables** box and click **OK** to run the test.

Screenshot 6.6

If the data does not satisfy the conditions for a parametric test then you should conduct the Wilcoxon test by going to the menu at the top of the screen and clicking: **Analyze / Nonparametric Tests / 2 Related Samples**. And then, as you have done above, highlight *both* variables and move them into the **Test Pair(s) List**. Ensure there is a tick next to Wilcoxon and click **OK** to run the test.

6.4 Summary

In this chapter you have learnt about:

- Independent and dependent variables.
- Hypothesis testing (experimental and null hypotheses) and the importance of considering confounding variables.
- How to select the appropriate statistical test for comparing differences between two sets of scores.

- The difference between independent samples and related samples, and between parametric and non-parametric data.
- How to produce histograms to check for normal distributions and statistical 'tests of normality'.
- How to produce an Independent samples t-test and interpret the results (including confidence intervals).
- How to produce the Mann-Whitney U test for non-parametric data.

In the following exercises you will also learn:

- How to compute a new variable from existing variables.

6.5 Exercises

Exercise 6.1 Checking for other significant differences

In this chapter we have concentrated on the differences in satisfaction ratings and number of sessions for the two counsellors. You may now wish to see if there were any significant differences in:

(a) the age of patients seen by the two counsellors;
(b) satisfaction ratings from male and female patients;
(c) the number of sessions conducted for male and female patients;
(d) the age of the male and female patients.

Remember to check the distribution of the data in order to run the appropriate analysis (i.e., parametric t-test or non-parametric Mann-Whitney U test).

Exercise 6.2 Create a new variable to analyse same-sex satisfaction ratings

In Chapter 4, cross-tabulation revealed that the majority of male patients (71%) saw John, while the majority of female patients (75%) saw Jane. We noted that this might be important information for the doctor, since this might suggest it is necessary to ensure a male and a female counsellor are available to cater for patient preferences, that is, preference for same-sex patient and counsellor.

Now, the curious among you might go on to wonder if this has any bearing on the counselling relationship, for example: were satisfaction ratings higher for same-sex patient–counsellor sessions compared to different-sex patient–counsellor sessions?

So how would you investigate this? Here is a clue: you will first need to create a new variable (using **Transform/Compute**) which records whether the patient saw a counsellor of the same sex or not. Then you can use this new variable as an independent (grouping) variable to compare the mean satisfaction ratings between the two groups.

6.6 Notes

1 Less commonly, related samples might be people who have been matched or paired on relevant criteria. And SPSS actually uses the term 'paired samples' for t-tests, rather than 'related samples'. Other terms for related samples include 'repeated measures' and 'dependent samples'.

2 While it is important to orientate towards these assumptions, studies have shown that parametric tests are actually quite robust to 'moderate departures' from these conditions (Howell 1997; Bryman and Cramer 2001).

3 You can obtain the median values by going to: **Analyze** then **Compare Means** then **Means**. In the **Means** box put **sessions** in the **Dependent List** and **counsellor** in the **Independent List**. Next, click on **Options** where you will see a list of statistics available; select **median** and move it to the **Cell Statistics** box, click **Continue**, then **OK**.

7 Reporting the results and presenting the data

In this final chapter we will look at how to structure the report of a quantitative study and how not to present data.

7.1 Introduction

Congratulations, you have done the easy bit – analysing the data – now comes the difficult part: writing-up the results.

Overall, the key criteria for good scientific writing are accuracy, clarity and structure, but you should also try to make it an interesting story, rather than a 'dry' listing of statistics and outcomes. In order to achieve clarity, you might imagine that you have been commissioned to produce the report for a professional who knows very little about the subject or research methods – in this case the doctor who has asked you to analyse the data. As regards structuring the report, fortunately, there are established guidelines on how to organize the results of a research study.

7.2 Structuring the report

A quantitative research report should generally include the following sections:

1 Abstract.
2 Introduction.
3 Methods.
4 Results.
5 Discussion.
6 Conclusion.
7 Appendices.
8 References.

The abstract

An abstract is a brief, concise summary of a study, usually limited to 200–300 words. It is usually the last part of the report to be written (since you need to know what you have said in order to provide the summary), and should include the following information:

- brief background to the research;
- purpose/aims of the study;
- methods used and the sample;
- brief conclusions outlining the importance of the study.

The role of the abstract is to give the reader sufficient information about the study, the essential details, to enable them to decide if they wish to read the full report.

The introduction

The introduction should provide a background to the research, specify the issue that is being addressed and review relevant previous research. For studies relating to health and social care, relevant policy documents are often cited to situate the study in the wider health and social context, with some indication of the extent of the problem. This approach is illustrated in the (rather excellent) example provided in Box 7.1.

The introduction may then close by outlining the aims and objectives of the study (research questions, hypotheses) if these have not been dealt with in a separate section.

Box 7.1 Introductions in health and social care: positioning the issue in a social context

This example is taken from Peter Greasley and Neil Small (2005a), evaluating a primary care counseling service: outcomes and issues, *Primary Health Care Research and Development*, 6: 125–31.

Introduction

Mental health issues are the third most common reason for consulting a general practitioner (GP), after respiratory disorders and cardiovascular disorders (Department of Health, 1991; Hemmings, 2000). A quarter of routine GP consultations relate to people with a mental health problem, most commonly depression and anxiety. It has been estimated that each year, one in 15 women and one in 30 men will be affected by depression, and every GP will see between 60 and 100 people with depression (Department of Health, 1999). A survey of 325 GPs conducted by the Mental Health After Care Association in 1999 found that 30% of their time, roughly 1.5 days a week, is spent working on patients' mental health problems, particularly relating to anxiety and depression (Davidson, 2000). The direct costs of treating depression in the UK in the early 1990s was estimated to be around £400 million a year and the indirect costs, including mortality costs and lost productivity was £3000 million (Kendrick, 2002).

Standard two of the National Service Framework for mental health (Department of Health, 1999) states that: 'Any service user who contacts their primary health care team with a common mental health problem should: 1) have their mental health needs identified and assessed; 2) be offered effective treatments, including referral to specialist services for further assessment, treatment and care if they require it' (p. 28). To achieve this, primary care groups/trusts (PCG/Ts) should 'develop the resources within each practice to assess mental health needs' (p. 35).

During the past 20 years counselling as a specific undertaking has been introduced into primary care, and the last decade has seen a rapid expansion . . .

The introduction then leads onto a review of studies reporting evaluations of counseling services in primary care and the evaluation reported in this study.

Methods

The key to the methods section is clarity and specificity, such that a reader could replicate the method and procedure of your study from the information you provide in the report. So we are talking about a very detailed account which should cover:

1 *Study design*: What is the overall methodology or design of the study? For example, is it an experiment (with independent and dependent variables), a questionnaire study, a qualitative study consisting of a series of interviews or focus groups, etc.?
2 *The participants*: What is the sampling frame (target sample, e.g., all patients who attend for counselling during one year at a general practice), sampling method (random, quota, all) and sample size? This may need to include demographic information (age, sex, ethnic background, etc.).
3 *The materials*: What materials were used in the study to conduct the research and collect data? For example, details of a questionnaire or other outcome measures may be provided in an appendix. If you are using a standardized outcome measure, for example, to measure health and quality of life, you should also provide details of its relevance to your particular study including details of reported reliability and validity (reliability refers to the consistency of the measure over time or with different samples; validity refers to the extent to which it measures what it is supposed to be measuring, e.g., levels of anxiety or depression).
4 *The procedure*: How was the study actually conducted? For example, if the study involved a questionnaire, how was it distributed to participants? Was it posted to participants who completed it then returned it, or was it completed in the presence of the researcher? (Studies have shown that the way in which a questionnaire is administered – self-completion, interview, etc. – can influence the responses (Lyons *et al.* 1999)). Remember, the reader should be able to replicate your procedure based on the details you provide in the report.

Results

The results should be presented as simply and clearly as possible. Make use of graphs and tables that help to present and explain the results. Where descriptive and inferential statistics are used to analyse the data, you should:

- name the statistic used;
- report the statistical significance of the results obtained;
- indicate that all necessary assumptions were met (e.g., that data were normally distributed if using a t-test).

It is also important for the report to have a logical structure. A good way to do this is to pose research questions or hypotheses which are then either confirmed or not by the data. You can then add words and phrases like 'surprisingly', 'as expected' or 'as predicted' when presenting the results of analysis. This makes the text more interesting than simply listing a ream of analyses; it turns the report into a story with twists and turns.

Graphs, figures and tables should be comprehensible without reference back to the text, so they should be clearly numbered and headed, and fully labelled with all units of measurement. They should only be included where they serve to enhance understanding of the results. Within the text you should lead the reader through the table or figure drawing attention to the relevant data. The reader should not turn the page and suddenly be confronted with a figure floating in the air: introduce the figure in the text and then explain it.

If you detect a note of frustration here, you would be correct. It comes from marking numerous assignments where these guidelines have been ignored; I have included some examples of charts from past assignments in the final section of this chapter which serve to illustrate how *not* to present data.

Discussion

The discussion section should provide an interpretation and explanation of the results which should be related to any research questions or hypotheses. It should also include critical reflections on the study (e.g., design of the questionnaire, relevance of outcome measures, limitations for generalizing due to small sample sizes).

Conclusion

The conclusion should include general implications of the study and suggestions or recommendations for further research.

Appendices

These should include any instruments used – such as the questionnaire.

References

A full list of references should be included (written in the appropriate academic style). This shows that you have consulted the relevant literature and acknowledged the sources of your work. It also enables the reader to consult the work you have cited if they wish.

7.3 How *not* to present data

Here are some examples of how not to present data. They are actual examples taken from assignments presented by students from previous years of teaching quantitative data analysis. The dataset involved analysing information from a group of students, including their age, height and whether they were full-time or part-time students.

Exhibit A

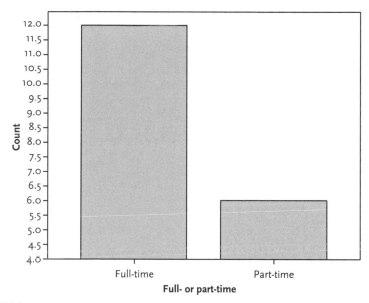

GRAPH I

What's wrong with this?

Well, first, it is very deceptive. If the purpose of including a chart is to provide a visual representation of the results which accurately reflects the data at a glance, then this chart is not the finest of examples.

It shows the number of full-time and part-time students on a course. If we were to just glance at the two bars it would appear that there are at least three times as many full-time students as there are part-time. But if you look at the Y-axis, you will see that there are actually only twice as many: six part-time and 12 full-time. The problem here is that the Y-axis starts at four.

The second problem is that the increments rise at intervals of 0.5. Is it possible to have half a student? The Y-axis should have been changed in the Chart Editor.

And, third, although the graph is numbered below (GRAPH 1), there is no title, for example, 'Graph 1: Number of students who are full-time and part-time'.

Exhibit B

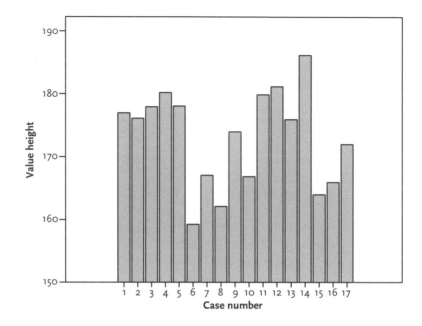

What's wrong with this?

There are many things wrong with this chart:

1 The chart is not numbered – neither is there a title.
2 The Y-axis (height) has no label of the actual measurements (centimetres).
3 The Y-axis starts at 150cms. Is case 14 really four times as tall as case 6?
4 The height should be ordered from lowest to highest.

But more generally, was it really necessary to produce a graph of each individual's height anyway?

Exhibit C

sex

		Frequency	Percent	Valid Percent	Cumulative Percent
Valid	male	8	47.1	47.1	47.1
	female	9	52.9	52.9	100.0
	Total	17	100.0	100.0	

sex

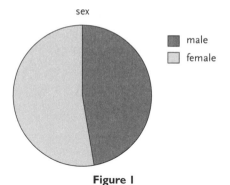

■ male
□ female

Figure 1

What's wrong with this?

Aside from the fact that neither a table nor a chart was really necessary to illustrate the fact that there were eight males and nine females – there are a number of other problems:

1   Neither the table nor the pie chart has titles – they are just labelled Figure 1.
2   Patterns rather than shaded areas should be used in pie charts and bar charts since most reports are published in black and white and the colour variations can become indistinguishable.
3   There are no numbers or percentages with the pie chart (though the table does provide these).

Exhibit D

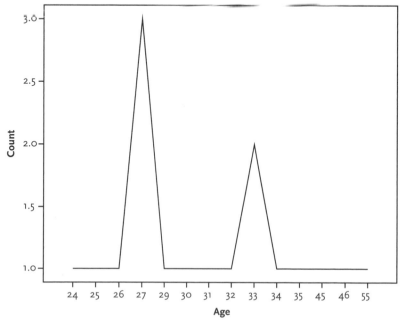

Figure 1

What's wrong with this?

Well, first, a line graph is inappropriate because it suggests continuous data rather than distinct age categories. It should be a bar chart.

Second, for some reason the Y-axis is at 0.5 intervals – there are no half-people!

And, third, the chart has no title – just 'Figure 1'.

Exhibit E

Full-Part-time status

This bar graph illustrates the frequency distribution of full-part-time status

N=1 (6%) respondents work/study part-time

N=16 (94%) respondents work/study full-time.

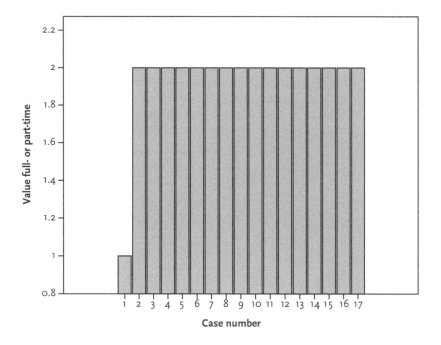

What's wrong with this?

Aside from the questionable value of graphically representing this data, look at the scale . . . What does it represent?!

Concluding remarks

My primary aim in writing this book has been to provide a relatively simple and accessible introduction to quantitative data analysis. It is for this reason that I have taken a pragmatic approach which skips much of the theoretical underpinnings of statistics in favour of practically conducting the analysis. For those students who will be taking their studies further, I would strongly recommend complementing this practical book with further reading around the principles of statistical analysis. A little knowledge of statistics can be a 'dangerous' thing, and this practical introduction to quantitative data analysis has merely scraped the surface in terms of the underlying principles.

I have one final word of warning. Many students design research studies without properly thinking through how they will analyse the data (I've done it myself of course – and paid the price). My advice to students is always to keep the design of your research study as simple as possible, and to stick to what you know: that is, design the study around the tests you know how to use. If you cannot do that then at least make sure you understand the test and the analyses that you are considering by consulting the relevant text books. Do not make the analyses an after-thought: design your study in haste, repent at leisure . . .

But the good thing of course, is that having worked through this book you now have the ability to understand and conduct what are probably the most commonly used statistics in health and social studies. Have fun . . .

Answers to the quiz and exercises

Chapter 1

Exercise 1.1 Types of data

Would the following variables yield interval or nominal/categorical data?

(a) ethnic background;
(b) student assignment marks;
(c) level of education;
(d) patient satisfaction ratings on a 1–7 scale.

Answers

(a) This would be nominal/categorical data since any numbers you assigned to the categories are arbitrary codes, e.g., Black–Caribbean (1); Black–African (2); Indian (3); etc.
(b) Student assignment marks, provided as percentages, are interval since they represent equal intervals on a 1–100 per cent scale.
(c) Levels of education would normally be considered as ordinal since they represent different levels of education on a scale, e.g., Diploma (1); Degree (2); Masters (3); MPhil (4); PhD (5). If you were to assign numbers to each of these categories, as I have done here, they would be more than arbitrary codes with the implication that (2) is a higher level of academic achievement than (1), and so on.
(d) Patient satisfaction ratings on a 1–7 scale may be regarded as interval data since the scale is presented in equal intervals (though strictly speaking, we should say that the rating scale is at least ordinal and approximates interval data).

Exercise 1.2 Measures of central tendency

Which do you imagine would be the most representative measure of central tendency for the following data?

(a) number of days for students to return overdue library books;
(b) IQ scores for a random sample of the population;
(c) number of patients cured of migraine in a year by an acupuncturist;
(d) number of counselling sessions attended by patients.

Answers

(a) Probably median – because most students will return overdue books within a few days – but some may not return them for weeks, months or years!

(b) This should be the mean since IQ scores should be normally distributed around a standardized mean of 100.

(c) None – this is categorical data! You would simply count the frequencies.

(d) Depends if the number of sessions were normally distributed (mean) or distinctly skewed by a few patients (median).

Exercise 1.3 Correlation

What sort of correlation would you expect to see from the following variables?

(a) fuel bills and temperature;
(b) ice cream sales and temperature;
(c) number of counselling sessions and gender.

Answers

(a) Negative: the cost of fuel bills *increases* as temperature *reduces* (and vice versa).[1]

(b) Positive: as temperature increases so does consumption of ice cream.

(c) None! This data would not be appropriate for correlation because we do not have two interval variables. Rather, we would be comparing the mean number of counselling sessions undertaken by males with those undertaken by females.

Exercise 1.4 Independent and dependent variables

Identify the independent and dependent variables in the following research questions:

(a) Does alcohol affect a person's ability to calculate mathematical problems?
(b) Is acupuncture better than physiotherapy in treating back pain?

Answers

(a) The independent variable (IV) is whether the person has taken alcohol or not. The experimenter might test this hypothesis by administering increasing amounts of alcohol: one bottle of whisky; two bottles of whisky; etc. The dependent variable (DV) is performance on the maths test.

(b) IV = treatment type (acupuncture or physiotherapy); DV = level of back pain.

Exercise 1.5 What type of analysis?

What type of analysis would you perform to examine the following?

(a) relationship between gender and preference for a cat or dog as a pet;

(b) relationship between time spent on an assignment and percentage mark;

(c) relationship between gender and patient satisfaction ratings.

Answers

(a) Since we have two nominal/categorical variables we should use cross-tabulation.

(b) Since we have two interval variables we should use correlation to see if time and marks are positively or negatively related.

(c) Since we have a categorical variable (gender) and an interval variable (ratings) we should use a test to compare the mean ratings of men and women.

Chapter 3

Exercise 3.1

You have already produced a histogram for the variable age. Now produce histograms illustrating the distribution of sessions and satisfaction ratings. What sort of distribution do they display? Is the data 'normally distributed'?

Answers

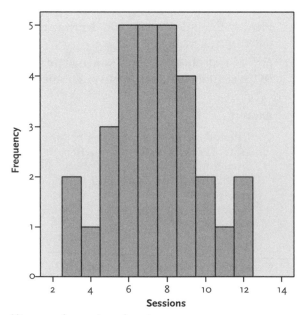

Figure X3.1a Histogram for number of sessions

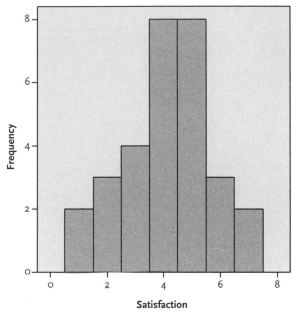

Figure X3.1b Histogram for satisfaction ratings

Both histograms show a relatively normal distribution with the majority of scores in the middle generally tailing off at either end of the scale.

Exercise 3.2

Produce boxplots comparing satisfaction ratings according to the gender of patients. What do you conclude from the results in terms of: (a) the spread of the data for males compared to females; (b) the relative satisfaction ratings of males compared to females?

Answers

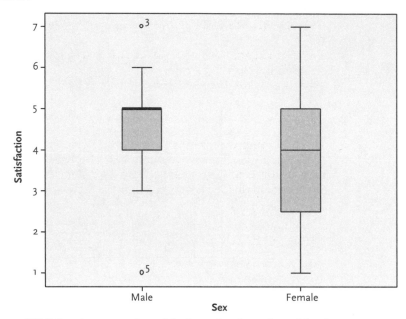

Figure X3.2 Boxplots comparing satisfaction ratings for males and females

From the boxplots above the first point we should note is that male patients were more satisfied with the counselling: they generally provide higher satisfaction ratings with a median rating of 5 compared to 4 for the female patients. On the 7 point rating scale, this would suggest that male patients were generally satisfied with the counselling service whereas for female patients this cannot be concluded. The larger spread of satisfaction ratings across female patients suggests a greater degree of ambivalence in the ratings, with some patients satisfied, but others not satisfied.

The fact that there are two outliers for the male satisfaction ratings reflects the relatively high degree of clustering for the majority of ratings (as illustrated by the middle 50 per cent of ratings in the boxplot).[2]

Incidentally, does your boxplot chart look like this one? I made a number of changes to the default chart by double-clicking on the Y-axis and making some alterations to the scale:

- I changed the minimum value to 1 (it was 0) – because the satisfaction scale actually goes from 1 to 7.
- I changed the major increment to 1 (it was 2) so we can see every value of the satisfaction scale.
- I increased the lower margin from 0 per cent to 5 per cent (to provide a gap between the 1 on the Y-axis and the X-axis).

Presentation is important, as noted earlier.

Chapter 4

Exercise 4.1 Recoding counselling sessions into categories

Recode the data for number of counselling sessions into three equal groups representing 'low', 'medium' and 'high' attendance, and first cross-tabulate with 'counsellor' then with 'sex'. What do these cross-tabulations show?

Answers

The first thing we need to know is the range of counselling sessions. From section 2 in Chapter 3 we know that the number of counselling sessions ranged from 3 to 12 (running a simple frequencies analysis will confirm this). So we should divide the sessions into the following three categories:

1 Low: 1–4 sessions.
2 Medium: 5–8 sessions.
3 High: 9–12 sessions.

Now that we know our categories we can re-code counselling sessions in SPSS using **Transform / Recode into Different Variables** and then cross-tabulate counsellor with our new variable.

Table X4.1b Counsellor / session categories cross-tabulation

counsellor * Session categories Crosstabulation

			Session categories			
			1-4	5-8	9-12	Total
counsellor	John	Count	1	6	7	14
		% within counsellor	7.1%	42.9%	50.0%	100.0%
	Jane	Count	2	12	2	16
		% within counsellor	12.5%	75.0%	12.5%	100.0%
Total		Count	3	18	9	30
		% within counsellor	10.0%	60.0%	30.0%	100.0%

From this cross-tabulation we can see that John tended to hold a larger number of sessions: 50 per cent of his patients attended for between 9–12 sessions compared to only 12 per cent of Jane's patients, the majority of whom (75 per cent) attended for between 5–8 sessions.

This would be useful information for our doctor who might be interested to know why half of John's patients were offered well above the recommended six sessions while Jane appears to be abiding by the recommendations. While there may be valid reasons for the extra number of sessions provided by John, the concern for the doctor may lie in resource implications: if John is spending too much time with his patients, the waiting time for referrals may go up.

You should then have gone on to cross-tabulate sessions with sex, resulting in the following table:

Table X4.1c Sex/session categories cross-tabulation

sex * Session categories Crosstabulation

			Session categories			
			1-4	5-8	9-12	Total
sex	male	Count	1	7	6	14
		% within sex	7.1%	50.0%	42.9%	100.0%
	female	Count	2	11	3	16
		% within sex	12.5%	68.8%	18.8%	100.0%
Total		Count	3	18	9	30
		% within sex	10.0%	60.0%	30.0%	100.0%

Here we can see that the main difference is again in the 9–12 category: 43 per cent of males attended for 9–12 sessions compared to only 19 per cent of the females. But of course, this may simply reflect the fact that the majority of male patients saw John. Or perhaps the fact that they are male patients has some bearing on the larger number of sessions needed? Whatever reasons there are for these results, if the doctor has the information clearly provided by you, he can then explore the reasons in discussion with the two counsellors.

Notes on conducting this exercise:

1   Did you include values labels as I have done – labelling the new categories 1–4, 5–8, 9–12? Students often fail to add these values labels, which are necessary to know what the categories represent. Alternatively, you might have labelled the categories 'low', 'medium' and 'high' – but these labels are more ambiguous than providing the actual ranges of each category.
2   Did you include row percentages? Although the numbers are low in each category you should include percentages, and they should be row percentages: some students include column percentages which are not appropriate since we want to know the relative number of sessions provided by each of the counsellors.

Exercise 4.2 Re-code satisfaction ratings into categories

Re-code the data for satisfaction ratings into categories representing 'positive', 'negative' and 'neutral' ratings. Cross-tabulate this new variable with 'counsellor' then 'sex'. What is the best way to categorize satisfaction ratings into these categories? What do these cross-tabulations show?

Answers

There have been a number of occasions in the past when I have found it useful to re-code scales like this into simpler categories for ease of interpretation. The first thing that we should note is that our satisfaction scale goes from 1–7:

Not at all satisfied   1 2 3 4 5 6 7   Very satisfied

Now, imagine if you were neither satisfied nor dissatisfied with the counselling, what number would you circle? Hopefully, if you are thinking the same as me, you would circle the number 4 because it lies in the dead centre of the scale – with three numbers to either side of it. So, if we accept that the number 4 can represent a 'neutral' attitude towards the counselling, then the numbers either side of it should represent a 'negative' attitude or a 'positive' attitude. Hence, if I was completing this rating scale I would circle the number 3 if I was mildly dissatisfied or the number 5 if I was mildly satisfied.

On this basis we can re-code the values as follows:

1 Negative (not satisfied): 1–3.
2 Neutral (neither satisfied nor dissatisfied): 4.
3 Positive (satisfied): 5–7.

When you have re-coded the satisfaction rating into these categories (**Transform / Recode into Different Variables**) and cross-tabulated with counsellor, your table should look like this:

Table X4.2b Counsellor/satisfaction categories cross-tabulation

counsellor * Satisfaction Categories Crosstabulation

			Satisfaction Categories			
			not satisfied	neutral	satisfied	Total
counsellor	John	Count	1	4	9	14
		% within counsellor	7.1%	28.6%	64.3%	100.0%
	Jane	Count	8	4	4	16
		% within counsellor	50.0%	25.0%	25.0%	100.0%
Total		Count	9	8	13	30
		% within counsellor	30.0%	26.7%	43.3%	100.0%

The main thing about interpreting these cross-tabulation tables is to look for the key differences – and they are pretty clear in this table. First, the majority of patients who saw John (64%) were satisfied, compared to only a quarter (25%) of Jane's patients. Second, 50% of Jane's patients were not satisfied, compared to only 7% of John's patients.

Although we cannot be certain as to the reasons for these levels of satisfaction, we should go on to consider other aspects of the data analysis that may throw some light on these results. For example, perhaps John received higher satisfaction ratings because he provided more sessions for his patients? In Chapter 6 we look at a test to examine this hypothesis.

We should then go on to cross-tabulate our satisfaction categories with the sex of the patients, and produce the following table:

Table X4.2c Sex/satisfaction categories cross-tabulation

sex * Satisfaction Categories Crosstabulation

			Satisfaction Categories			
			not satisfied	neutral	satisfied	Total
sex	male	Count	2	4	8	14
		% within sex	14.3%	28.6%	57.1%	100.0%
	female	Count	7	4	5	16
		% within sex	43.8%	25.0%	31.3%	100.0%
Total		Count	9	8	13	30
		% within sex	30.0%	26.7%	43.3%	100.0%

This cross-tabulation shows that the majority (57%) of male patients were satisfied compared to less than a third (31%) of female patients. Furthermore, only 14 per cent of male patients were dissatisfied, compared to 44 per cent of female patients.

But of course, the problem with this cross-tabulation is that it is confounded by the fact that most male patients saw John (and had more sessions). Perhaps at this point we need to be careful not to confuse the doctor with too many tables. . . .

Notes on conducting this exercise:

1 Aside from the importance of including row percentages, notice that I have included descriptive value labels ('not satisfied', etc.) rather than the actual ratings (1–3). This contradicts my advice in the previous exercise! However, on this occasion I felt that these descriptive labels were more informative than the numbers, but I would ensure that the ratings they represent, and the rationale for the re-coding was made clear in the report to the doctor so that he has all the information to decide for himself if this is a useful analysis of the data.
2 Some people may have a problem with this re-coding of the satisfaction scale since we cannot be certain that patients were responding in the way we have categorized the data. If you do decide to re-code data in this way you should present a clear rationale justifying your actions. Interestingly, many students who have completed this exercise choose to re-code the data into the following categories:

   - 1–2: negative (not satisfied).
   - 3–5: neutral (neither satisfied nor dissatisfied).
   - 6–7: positive (satisfied).

While this might be preferable in terms of distinguishing those patients who were truly satisfied from those who were not, the problem I have with this is the rationale for what the numbers 3–5 represent: can 3 really be put in the same category as 5?

Chapter 5

Exercise 5.1

Conduct correlations for (a) age and number of sessions; and (b) age and satis-faction with the service. Remember to produce a scatterplot for the data before running the Pearson correlation. What do the results show in terms of (a) the strength and direction of any correlations; and (b) the statistical significance of the results?

Answers

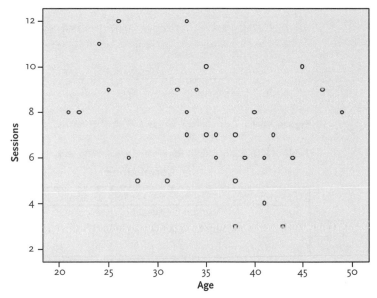

Figure X5.1a Correlations for age and number of sessions

Table X5.1a Correlations for age and number of sessions

Correlations

		age	sessions
age	Pearson Correlation	1	-.285
	Sig. (2-tailed)		.127
	N	30	30
sessions	Pearson Correlation	-.285	1
	Sig. (2-tailed)	.127	
	N	30	30

From the scatterplot we can see that there appears to be a slight negative relationship between age and the number of sessions. This is supported by the Pearson product moment correlation coefficient which found a slight negative correlation, although this was not statistically significant: $r = -.28$, $p = .127$.

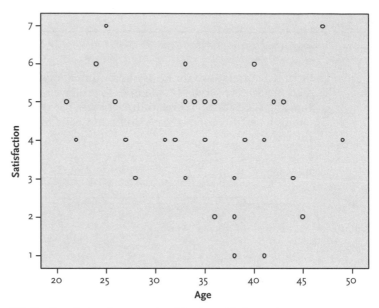

Figure X5.1b Correlations for age and satisfaction with the service

Table X5.1b Correlations for age and satisfaction with the service

Correlations

		age	satisfaction
age	Pearson Correlation	1	-.234
	Sig. (2-tailed)		.214
	N	30	30
satisfaction	Pearson Correlation	-.234	1
	Sig. (2-tailed)	.214	
	N	30	30

From the scatterplot we can see that there appears to be a slight negative correlation between age and level of satisfaction. This is supported by the Pearson product moment correlation coefficient which found a slight negative relationship, but this was not statistically significant: $r = -.23$, $p = .214$.

Note: In SPSS v15 you may need to use Chart Editor to change the Y-axis scale in order to provide a 5 per cent lower margin for the lower values.

Exercise 5.2 The importance of sample sizes in correlation

Sample sizes can have a profound effect on statistical significance. Try running the Pearson correlation between *age* and *number of sessions* again, but this time with double the number of cases for each of these variables.

Highlight the 30 cases for **age**, right-click the mouse button and copy, then move your cursor to the end of the data column for **age** (row 31) and paste in the data you have copied. So you have the same data but double the number of cases. Next, follow the same procedure for **sessions**. Then run the Pearson correlation on the 60 cases for ages and sessions.

Answers

When you run the Pearson correlation for these 60 cases for age and number of sessions this should produce the following output table:

Table X5.2 Correlations

Correlations

		age	sessions
age	Pearson Correlation	1	-.285*
	Sig. (2-tailed)		.028
	N	60	60
sessions	Pearson Correlation	-.285*	1
	Sig. (2-tailed)	.028	
	N	60	60

*. Correlation is significant at the 0.05 level (2-tailed).

Although the level of correlation remains the same as before (in exercise 5.1(a)) when there were only 30 cases, the result is now statistically significant: $r = -.285$, $p = 0.028$.

This is because obtaining statistical significance is to some extent dependent on sample size: larger samples are more likely to produce statistically significant results than smaller samples. This is particularly the case in correlation statistics where you might find that two variables from a small sample (e.g., less than 20) are strongly correlated – but the result is not statistically significant. Conversely, with a very large sample, it is possible to obtain significant results for very weak correlations. As Bryman and Cramer (2001: 176) point out, if you have approximately 500 cases, r only needs to be 0.088 to be significant at the 0.05 level, but with only 18 cases r will need to be at least 0.468.

It is of course one thing to find a statistically significant result, and another to find a meaningful result. This is relevant to our correlation between age and number of sessions for two reasons: (1) a correlation of −.285 suggests (if you square it) that 8.1 per cent of the variance in sessions is accounted for by age. Well, that is not much! It may be significant but it is not very meaningful; (2) even if the result did suggest that younger patients attended for more sessions, so what? This information *could* have some relevance, in certain circumstances, but the reason for conducting any analyses, and certainly if you are including them in a final report, needs to be justified, otherwise it becomes a list of meaningless analyses for the sake of it.

Exercise 5.3 The importance of 'outliers' in correlation

There is another reason why you should always produce a scatterplot of the data if you are looking for correlations: to identify outliers – any data points that are out on their own away from the main cluster. These can have a significant influence on any correlation statistics.

Have a look at the scatterplot for *age* and *satisfaction* again (you should have produced it for Exercise 5.1b). Are there any outliers? Imagine trying to draw an oval, fat cigar shape around the dots in the scatterplot to discern a negative correlation – is there one dot in particular that falls outside your oval shape? If so, identify the case number, remove it from your dataset (values for age and satisfaction), and run the Pearson correlation again.

Answers

I have reproduced the graph below with my oval, fat cigar shape superimposed to indicate a more discernible negative correlation, and the possible 'outlier' (top right):

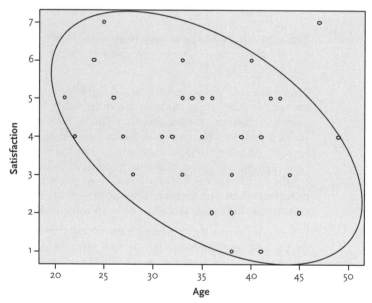

Figure X5.3a Scatterplot for age and satisfaction

The next step is to identify the outlier in our SPSS database. We can see that this is one of only two cases indicating a satisfaction rating of 7, and the age is about 47. Looking through the dataset we can identify this as case 20. Remove the values 7 (satisfaction rating) and 47 (age) for this case and run the Pearson correlation again. This should produce the output table below where we can see that the strength of the negative correlation is now –.377 (previously –.234) and is actually significant: p = .044.

Table X5.3a Correlations

Correlations

		age	satisfaction
age	Pearson Correlation	1	-.377*
	Sig. (2-tailed)		.044
	N	29	29
satisfaction	Pearson Correlation	-.377*	1
	Sig. (2-tailed)	.044	
	N	29	29

*. Correlation is significant at the 0.05 level (2-tailed).

Now obviously you need to be careful removing data like this – you cannot just remove data you do not like! The main point being, that outliers can have a dramatic effect on the value obtained for a correlation. For example, the following scatterplot provides data where there is no correlation between two variables.

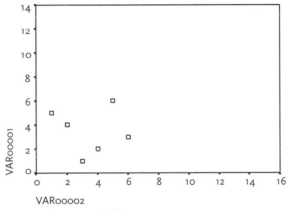

Figure X5.3b No correlation: r = −.086

However, when one extreme data point – an outlier – is added this turns into a strong positive correlation!

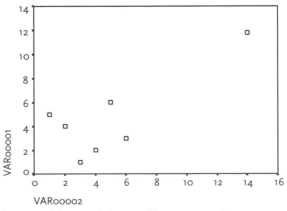

Figure X5.3c Strong positive correlation: r = .79

The moral is thus: always check your data for outliers (e.g., using boxplots) and always produce a scatterplot to visually examine the data before conducting a correlation statistical analysis.

Exercise 5.4 Explain the following correlations

(a) It is reported that there is a strong positive correlation between ice cream sales and crime rates. Do we therefore conclude that ice cream causes crime?

(b) It is reported that there is a positive correlation between number of counselling sessions and level of psychological well-being? Can we therefore conclude that counselling works and more counselling works better?

(c) Consumption of milk is positively correlated to cancer. So does drinking milk cause cancer?

(d) Studies have found a negative correlation between smoking and Alzheimer's dementia: the risk of getting Alzheimer's dementia reduces with increased smoking of cigarettes. Would you therefore recommend that people start smoking or increase the number they smoke to prevent the onset of Alzheimer's dementia?

Answers

(a) Well, unless there is something in the ice cream, it has probably got something to do with the temperature: more people are out when it is warm and sunny, more people are drinking, etc.

(b) Well, that *may* be the case but can we really be certain the improvement is due to the counselling? Perhaps there are other events in the patients' lives that have led to an improvement in well-being, or perhaps improvements reflect 'normal' readjustment over time after a particular trauma.
Imagine the opposite scernario: you measure psychological well-being for a sample of patients before and after counselling and find that it deteriorates. To make matters worse, you then find a negative correlation between the amount of counselling and psychological well-being. Would you then conclude that counselling makes people worse and that the more they have the worse they are?

(c) Another explanation might be that the greater level of consumption of milk is in wealthier countries, where people live longer and therefore become more susceptible to cancer.

(d) First, these studies were funded by the tobacco industry and the suggested implication was that smoking (or nicotine) may prevent the onset of Alzheimer's dementia. The problem is that Alzheimer's dementia is a disease of older people: 50 per cent of people older than 90 years are diagnosed with Alzheimer's. The findings may simply reflect the fact that heavy smokers do not live long enough to get Alzheimer's because they die younger of smoking-related diseases.

Chapter 6

Exercise 6.1 Checking for other significant differences

In this chapter we have concentrated on the differences in satisfaction ratings and number of sessions for the two counsellors. You may now wish to see if there are any significant differences in:

(a) the age of patients seen by the two counsellors;
(b) satisfaction ratings from male and female patients;
(c) the number of sessions conducted for male and female patients;
(d) the age of the male and female patients.

Remember to check the distribution of the data in order to run the appropriate analysis (i.e., parametric t-test or non-parametric Mann-Whitney U test).

Answers

For each of these exercises I found the parametric t-test to be appropriate, the results of which were as follows:

(a) The age of patients seen by the two counsellors:
  • mean age of patients seen by John = 32.8 years;
  • mean age of patients seen by Jane = 37.3 years;
  • t-test results: $t = -1.725$, $p = .096$. Not significant.
(b) Satisfaction ratings from male and female patients:
  • mean satisfaction rating for males: 4.57;
  • mean satisfaction rating for females: 3.75;
  • t-test results: $t = 1.457$, $p = .156$. Not significant.
(c) The number of sessions conducted for male and female patients:
  • mean number of sessions for male patients: 8.29;
  • mean number of sessions for female patients: 6.56;
  • t-test results: $t = 2.13$, $p = .042$.
  Thus, we can conclude that male patients attended for more sessions than females. However, is this because male patients for some reason require more sessions or because more patients saw John who tended to provide more sessions . . .?
(d) The age of the male and female patients:
  • mean age of male patients: 31.3 years;
  • mean age of female patients: 38.6 years;
  • t-test results: $t = -3.075$, $p = .005$.
  Thus, we can conclude that female patients were generally older than male patients. However, what bearing this might have on anything is unclear – not all significant differences are meaningful differences . . .

Exercise 6.2 Create a new variable to analyse same-sex satisfaction ratings

In Chapter 4, cross-tabulation revealed that the majority of male patients (71%) saw John, while the majority of female patients (75%) saw Jane. We noted that this might be important information for the doctor, since this might suggest it is necessary to ensure a male and a female counsellor are available to cater for patient preferences, that is, preference for same-sex patient and counsellor.

Now, the curious among you might go on to wonder if this has any bearing on the counselling relationship, for example: were satisfaction ratings higher for same-sex patient–counsellor sessions compared to different-sex patient–counsellor sessions?

So how would you investigate this? Here is a clue: you will first need to create a new variable (using **Transform/Compute**) which records whether the patient saw a counsellor of the same sex or not. Then you can use this new variable as an independent (grouping) variable to compare the mean satisfaction ratings between the two groups.

Answers

1 From the menu at the top of the screen go to **Transform/Compute Variable**.
2 In the **Target Variable** box enter a name for the new variable you are going to create. I have chosen the name '**samesex**'.
3 In the box **Numeric Expression** write in the rule you will need for the new variable to record whether the patient saw a counsellor of the same sex or not.

   In our data a male patient is coded as 1 and the male counsellor (John) is also coded as 1. Similarly, a female patient and the female counsellor (Jane) are both coded as 2. So, we need to select those cases where the *number* in the sex variable is the *same* as the number in the counsellor variable. This will tell us that we had a male patient and a male counsellor or a female patient and a female counsellor.

4 There are various ways to compute this, but the simplest is to enter: **sex = counsellor** in the **Numeric Expression** box.[3] This will create a new variable (samesex) showing those cases where the values were the same (and therefore also not the same) across the variables sex and counsellor.

Screenshot X6.2a

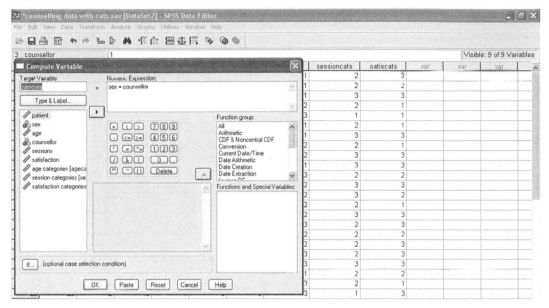

5 Click **OK** and your new variable (**samesex**) will appear in the **Data View** (I have removed decimal places):

Screenshot X6.2b

Having checked a few cases to see that this rule actually did what you wanted it to do, you can then compare satisfaction ratings for same-sex and different sex patient–counsellor.

(You might also realize at this point that it would have been simpler to do this without the Transform/Compute facility; that is, by simply creating the new variable and inserting a 1 where you can see that the counsellor and patient were of the same sex and a zero where they were not!)

Below I have conducted an independent t-test on the two groups, which shows no significant differences, but really the numbers are too small in the different sex patient counsellor group to conduct any significant analyses (just eight patients compared to 22 in the same-sex patient–counsellor group).

Table X6.2b Independent samples test

Group Statistics

	samesex	N	Mean	Std. Deviation	Std. Error Mean
satisfaction	different sex	8	3.75	1.669	.590
	same sex	22	4.27	1.549	.330

Table X6.2b Independent samples test

Independent Samples Test

		Levene's Test for Equality of Variances		t-test for Equality of Means						
									95% Confidence Interval of the Difference	
		F	Sig.	t	df	Sig. (2-tailed)	Mean Difference	Std. Error Difference	Lower	Upper
satisfaction	Equal variances assumed	.077	.784	-.802	28	.430	-.523	.652	-1.859	.813
	Equal variances not assumed			-.773	11.687	.455	-.523	.676	-2.000	.955

I have included this mainly as an academic exercise to illustrate the use of the Transform/Compute facility, since there have been a few occasions when students have needed to compute new values in their own data.

For example, the *SF-36 Health Survey* questionnaire (Ware *et al.* 2000) consists of 36 questions measuring various dimensions of health status such as:

1 Physical functioning (ten questions).
2 Mental health (five questions).
3 Energy/vitality (four questions).

When analysing scales such as this you would need to use the Transform/Compute facility to compute a new variable providing a mean score for the questions representing each dimension. So, in the example below I have used Transform/Compute to calculate the mean score from five mental health questions (mh1, mh2, etc.) which will then be produced in a new variable called 'mhmean'.

Screenshot X6.2c

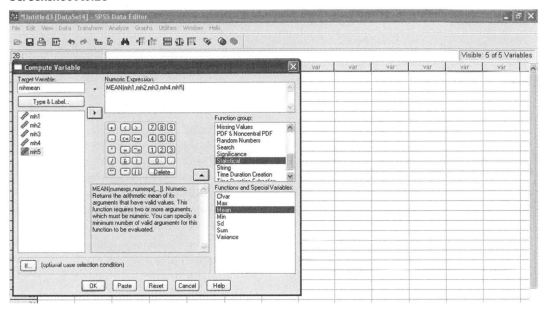

Notes

1 Of course, pedantic students will note, as they frequently do in my lectures, that if you are living in a country with a warm climate – then you may have a positive correlation. fuel bills may rise for air conditioning as temperature rises.

2 The two outliers identified in the boxplots are merely the lowest and highest scores on the seven point rating scale. In this respect the term 'outlier' may be deceptive with relatively restricted scales, and it should be remembered that boxplots are merely visual guides to the data (Howell 1997) that may, or may not, be instructive in checking the data.

3 Other ways to do this include: (1) using the not equal sign (~=) to select those cases where the numbers were not the same (different sex patient–counsellor); (2) writing out the rule in full: sex = 1 and counsellor = 1 or sex = 2 and counsellor = 2; (3) writing the rule: sex + counsellor = 3.

Glossary

ANOVA Analysis of variance (ANalysis Of VAriance) – a statistical technique normally used to examine differences between three or more samples/group means (compared to, for example, the T-test which examines differences for just two samples/group means).

categorical data This is data that represents different categories, rather than a scale, e.g., sex of patients, ethnic background.

chi-square A statistical test primarily associated with cross-tabulation to test for the 'independence' or 'association' between two categorical variables.

confidence intervals Where a mean difference in two samples is observed, 95 per cent confidence intervals provide lower and upper values around this mean difference with a 95 per cent probability that the true difference lies within these parameters.

confounding variables Essentially this refers to factors other than those under investigation that may have influenced outcomes of an experiment. More formally, these are variables other than the 'treatment' or 'independent' variable that may have affected the outcomes on the dependent variable. Sometimes referred to as extraneous variables, i.e., variables which may have influenced the outcomes but were not (or could not be) controlled by the experimenter.

continuous variable A variable measured on interval or ratio scales.

control group A separate sample used to compare outcomes with a sample subjected to an experimental treatment. For example, in a medical experiment the control group may be left untreated or given a placebo pill to compare outcomes with those receiving the treatment.

correlation A correlation assesses the relationship between two continuous variables to see if values on one variable vary in relation to the other, e.g., height and weight.

cross-tabulation Where two or more variables are presented in a table to compare relative frequencies across categories.

dependent variable A variable, the outcome of which is predicted to be *dependent* on allocation to the treatment or independent variable; for example, level of back pain (dependent variable) will depend on the type of treatment a patient was allocated to by the researcher (e.g., physiotherapy or acupuncture).

descriptive statistics Descriptive statistics provide summary information about data, for example, describing the sample in terms of age, gender and other characteristics. Measures of central tendency may be used along with graphs and other means of describing data.

extraneous variables See *confounding variables*.

frequencies The number of times a particular value is represented in a sample, e.g., the number of males and number of females.

hypothesis A prediction that is being tested.

independent samples t-test A statistical test used to determine whether the mean scores from two independent samples (e.g., males/females) differ significantly.

independent variable A term normally used in experimental design which refers to the variable manipulated by the researcher, e.g., assignment of patients to treatment A or treatment B. It is sometimes referred to as the treatment variable.

interval data This is data which takes the form of a scale in which the numbers go from low to high in equal intervals.

Mann-Whitney test A non-parametric statistical test to determine differences in two independent samples.

mean The arithmetic mean is the most common measure of central tendency and is produced by calculating the sum of the values and then dividing by the number of values.

measures of central tendency Measures of central tendency are used to provide the typical or average values for a sample of data, e.g., the mean age of the sample. The mean, median or mode may be used depending on the distribution of the data.

median A measure of central tendency which is the midpoint of an ordered distribution of values.

mode A measure of central tendency referring to the most frequently occurring value in a set of scores.

nominal data This is another term for categorical data, whereby discrete categories may be nominated a numerical code, e.g., code male as 1 and female as 2.

non-parametric test A statistical test which does not depend on the assumptions (parameters) required by parametric tests, e.g., normal distribution of data.

normal distribution A frequency distribution where the majority of values are in the middle of the range, tailing off at either end of the scale producing a symmetrical bell shaped curve.

null hypothesis This is the hypothesis that is proposed to be *nullified* or refuted, e.g., there will be no difference between the two samples.

one-tailed test A test where the hypothesis predicts an effect in one direction, e.g., predicting that levels of anxiety will *reduce* as a result of counselling (compared to a 2-tailed test which abstains from making a directional prediction, i.e., that counselling will have an effect on levels of anxiety - but we cannot be certain if this will lead to a reduction or increase in levels of anxiety).

ordinal data This is data that can be put into an ordered sequence. For example, the rank order of runners in a race – 1st, 2nd, 3rd.

outliers Data which lies outside the majority of scores.

parametric statistics Statistical tests that assume certain parameters of the data, e.g., a normal distribution.

power This relates to the power of a statistical test to detect a statistically significant effect/difference if there really is one. The power of a statistical test to detect a difference may depend on sample size (the larger the better) and the size of the effect/difference that is being investigated.

probability This refers to the likelihood of an event occurring by chance. If the event cannot happen the probability is zero; if the event is certain to happen the probability is one.

p value This refers to the probability of the outcomes occurring by chance, expressed numerically as ranging from zero to one. The convention is to accept a p value of 0.05 or less as being statistically significant, which translates to a probability of 1 in 20 of the results occurring by chance.

ratio scale A scale where points are separated by equal intervals with a true zero, e.g., height, weight, age, length.

regression analysis Regression analysis assesses the relationship between one or more dependent variables and independent variables in order to find a line that best predicts the relationship between the two. It is then possible to estimate values of a dependent variable from values of an independent variable.

related samples t-test A statistical test used to determine whether the mean scores from two related samples differ significantly.

repeated measures design Where two or more measures are taken from the same sample (in contrast to independent subjects design), e.g., levels of anxiety before and after counselling for a sample of patients.

standard deviation A measure of the amount of deviation from the mean in a sample of scores.

statistical significance An observation that is unlikely to have occurred by chance at a specified level of probability.

t-test A statistical technique for examining differences in means between two samples.

two-tailed test A test where the hypothesis does not specify a direction for the effect (non-directional), e.g., the treatment will have an effect but we cannot be certain if this will lead to an increase or decrease in patient ratings.

type I error Essentially, accepting a statistical difference/effect when there really is not one (like a false-positive). In more formal terms it refers to a rejection of the null hypothesis (no difference) when it is in fact true.

type II error Essentially, accepting the absence of a statistical difference or effect when there really is one (like a false-negative). In more formal terms, failing to reject the null hypothesis (no difference) when it should be rejected.

Wilcoxon test A non-parametric statistical test to determine differences in two related samples.

References

Argyrous, G. (2005) *Statistics for Research: With a Guide to SPSS*. London: Sage.

Bowling, A. (1997) *Research Methods in Health*. Buckingham: Open University Press.

Bryman, A. and Cramer, D. (2001) *Quantitative Data Analysis with SPSS Release 10 for Windows*. London: Routledge.

Cohen, J. (1988) *Statistical Power Analysis for the Behavioural Sciences*. Hillsdale, NJ: Erlbaum.

Coolidge, F. L. (2006) *Statistics: A Gentle Introduction*. London: Sage.

Davidson, L. (2000) Meeting the challenges of the new NHS for counselling in primary care: a service manager perspective. *British Journal of Guidance and Counselling* 28, 191–202.

Department of Health (1991) *The health of the nation white paper: point prevalence of mental disorders in the adult population (England)*, Section C. London: Her Majesty's Stationery Office.

Department of Health (1999) *A national service framework for mental health*. London: Her Majesty's Stationery Office.

Einspruch, E. L. (2005) *An Introductory Guide to SPSS for Windows*. London: Sage.

Field, A. (2005) *Discovering Statistics Using SPSS*. London: Sage.

Gravetter, F. J. and Wallnau, L. B. (2002) *Essentials of Statistics for the Behavioral Sciences*. Belmont, CA: Wadsworth.

Greasley, P. and Small, N. (2005a) Evaluating a primary care counselling service: outcomes and issues, *Primary Health Care Research & Development*, 6: 125–36.

Greasley, P. and Small, N. (2005b) Providing welfare advice in general practice: Referrals, issues and outcomes, *Health and Social Care in the Community*, 13: 249–58.

Hemmings, A. (2000) Counselling in primary care: a review of the practice evidence. *British Journal of Guidance and Counselling* 28, 233–52.

Howell, D. (1997) *Statistical Methods for Psychology*. London: Duxbury Press.

Huff, D. (1991) *How to Lie with Statistics*. London: Penguin.

Jamieson, S. (2004) Likert scales: how to (ab)use them. *Medical Education*, 38: 1212–8.

Kendrick, T. (2002) Depression. In Marshall, M.(Ed) *Quality indicators for general practice*. London: Royal Society of Medicine Press, 28–37.

Kinnear, P. and Gray, C. (2004) *SPSS 12 Made Simple*. Hove: Psychology Press.

Lyons, R.A., Wareham, K. and Lucas, M., Price, D., Williams, J. and Hutchings, H. (1999) SF-36 scores vary by method of administration: implications for study design, *Journal of Public Health Medicine*, 21: 41–5.

Pallant, J. (2001) *SPSS Survival Manual*. Buckingham: Open University Press.

Pell, G. (2005) Use and misuse of Likert scales. *Medical Education*, 39: 970.

Pett, M. (1997) *Nonparametric statistics for health care research*, London: Sage.

Robson, C. (1973) *Experiment, Design and Statistics in Psychology*. London: Penguin.

Robson, C. (2002) *Real World Research*. Oxford: Blackwell.

Ware, J. E., Kosinski, M. and Dewey, J. E. (2000) *Version 2 of the SF-36 Health Survey*. Lincoln, RI: Quality Metric Inc.

Watson, R., Atkinson, I. and Egerton, P. (2006) *Successful Statistics for Nursing & Healthcare*. Hampshire: Palgrave Macmillan.

Wood, M. (2003) *Making Sense of Statistics: A Non-Mathematical Approach*. Hampshire: Palgrave Macmillan.

Index